# PAINT
# WITHOUT BRUSHES

## Create with a wide variety of paints, props, textures and supplies.

**SPECIAL THANKS TO**
Kristi Franseen and Dawn Zavodsky
for sharing painting experiences
which their classes of young children
have enjoyed over the years.
May your children enjoy them too!

# PAINT WITHOUT BRUSHES

by
Liz & Dick Wilmes

Illustrations by
Tim McGinnis

A **Building Blocks** Publication

38W567 Brindlewood, Elgin, Illinois   60123

## ART

Cover Design and Computer Graphics          David Van Delinder
                                            Studio 155
                                            Elgin, IL   60120

Text Illustration                           Tim McGinnis

**PUBLISHED BY:**
BUILDING BLOCKS
38W567 Brindlewood
Elgin, IL 60123                             ISBN 0-943452-15-5

Go beyond the paint
jar and brush to
encourage children to
explore the world
of paint.

# Contents

## APPENDICES

# Adhesive Tape Painting

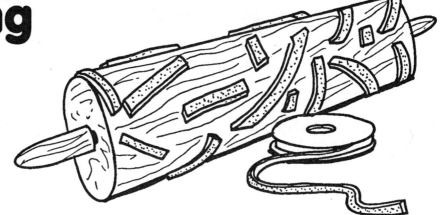

## Materials

Several rolling pins
Self-adhesive, foam
insulation tape
Large meat trays
Tempera paint
Butcher paper

## Preparation

✓ Cut different lengths of insulation tape. Adhere the strips in random patterns to the rolling pins.

✓ Pour shallow amounts of different colors of paint onto the meat trays.

✓ Put one or two rolling pins with each color of paint.

✓ Cut the butcher paper the length of your art table.

## Activity

Lay the butcher paper on the art table/floor. Set the paint and textured rolling pins around the edges of the paper.

Let the children roll the rolling pins in the paint and then onto the butcher paper. Keep rolling, using the different pins and colors of paint. Let the paint dry and then hang your mural for everyone to see.

11

# All Color Mix Fingerpainting

## Materials

Different colors of fingerpaint including black and white
Small containers
Small spoons
Plastic trays

## Preparation

✓ Spoon different colors of fingerpaint into small containers. Add a spoon to each one.

### Color Mix Ideas

Yellow and red
Green and red
Yellow and blue
Red and blue
Any color plus white and vice versa
Any color plus black and vice versa
Green with yellow and blue
Red with blue and yellow
Blue with black and orange
All colors

## Activity

Put the containers of paint and plastic trays on the art table. When children want to fingerpaint have them spoon paint onto their trays and have fun moving and mixing the paints. Encourage them to add more paint or a different color of paint. What happens?

# Blow Painting

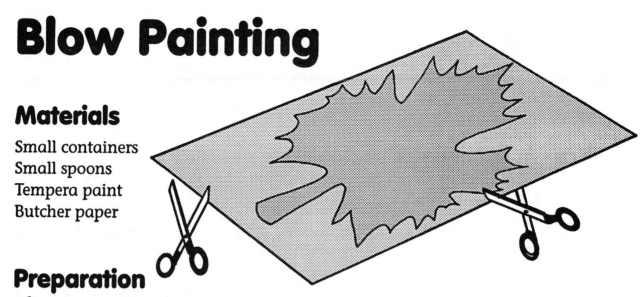

## Materials

Small containers
Small spoons
Tempera paint
Butcher paper

## Preparation

✓ Water-down the different colors of tempera paint until they are very watery. Pour the paint into small containers.

✓ Put a spoon in each container.

✓ Cut butcher paper into giant shapes.

## Activity

Lay one or two giant shapes on the art table/floor. Tape them down. Set the paint containers near the shapes.

Have the children spoon small puddles of paint onto the shapes, and then, pretending that they are the wind, blow the paint around. Spoon more paint and blow some more. Encourage the children to blow softly like gentle breezes and hard like fierce winds. Let the paintings dry and then hang them around the room.

13

# Body Printing

## Materials

Small meat trays
Paper towels
Tempera paint
Construction paper

## Preparation

✓ Make different colored printing pads. To make each pad:

  **1.** Fold several paper towels together so that they form a thick pad which fits on a meat tray.

  **2.** Set the paper towel pad on the meat tray. Slowly pour one color of paint over the pad. Let the paint soak in. Pour more if necessary. You want the pad to be moist but not soggy.

  **3.** Repeat the process for each printing pad.

## Activity

Set the printing pads and construction paper on the table. Let the children make prints using any parts of their bodies they'd like — fingers, elbows, knuckles, wrists, knees, etc. Encourage them to try different parts. (Add more paint to your printing pads as necessary.)

After each child has finished, have him tell you how he made some of his prints. Label them.

# Boot Painting

## Materials

5-6 pairs of children's boots
Tempera paint
Brownie pans
White butcher paper

## Preparation

✓ Cut the piece of butcher paper into 3-4 giant circles.

✓ Fill each brownie pan with a little tempera.

## Activity

Lay at least two of the giant circles on the floor in the art area. Put the boots on newspaper or an old rug next to the circles. Set the pans of paint next to the boots.

Have each child take off his shoes, choose boots, and put them on. Help him step into a pan of paint, wiggle the boots around to get the bottoms full of of color, and then step onto one of the circles. Let him walk around on the circle/s for as long as he'd like. Maybe he'll need to come back and step into the paint again.

When he's finished his walk have him take off his boots, put them back, and put his shoes on.

# Broom Painting

## Materials

Child-size brooms
Large pails
Food coloring

## Preparation

✓ None

## Activity

Have the children fill the pails about half full of water. You and the children carry the pails to the concrete or sidewalk and set them down. Let the children dip the brooms in the water and then Broom Paint with giant broom strokes.

On another warm day add food coloring to the water and Broom Paint with colored water. Another time color the water with powdered tempera paint. Be sure to always rinse the pavement before going inside. While Broom Painting talk about the different paints.

16

# Bubble Blow Printing

## Materials

Large mixing bowl
Water
Liquid dish detergent
Food coloring
Wide-mouth straws
Waste basket
White butcher paper

## Preparation

✓ Pour water into pitchers which children can easily handle.

✓ Cut the butcher paper into different shapes/sizes which will nicely hang in your sunny windows.

✓ Put the detergent, food coloring, and straws on a tray.

✓ Set the waste basket near the table.

## Activity

Set the water pitchers, large bowl, paper, and tray of supplies on the art table. Let the children help you mix the simple bubble brew. First pour the water into the bowl until it is about 3/4 full. Add several 'squirts' of detergent and then one color of food coloring such as red.

Let the children use straws to blow the bubble mixture until the bubbles are overflowing the bowl. Have several children hold a piece of paper over the bubbles so that it barely touches them. As the bubbles burst, slowly lower the paper until the bubbles are gone. Blow the bubbles again into a giant 'bubble mound.' Hold the paper on the bubbles and slowly print them again. Repeat several more times. Add a second color to the mixture and continue blowing and printing the bubbles. Add a third color if you'd like.

When you have finished printing each one hold it up to the sun or light and look at the beautiful translucent colors. Hang the Bubble Blow Prints in your windows.

# Bubble Blowing At The Easel

## Materials

Commercial bubble
blowing mixtures
Food coloring
Paper towels
Bubble wands
Easel paper

## Preparation

✓ Pour a different color of food
  coloring into each bottle of
  bubbles.

✓ Put newspaper under the
  easel to catch bubbles which
  burst before hitting the easel
  paper.

## Activity

Put the bottles of bubbles in the
easel trays. Have the children clip
paper to the easel and blow
colored bubbles at the paper.
Encourage them to blow slowly
and watch the bubbles pop on
their papers.

**HINT:** *When the bubbles
burst on the paper, the
solution sprays a little and
might splash onto the
child's cheeks. Have paper
towels close by so that
they can wipe their
faces when they are
done.*

18

# Bubble Pack Fingerpainting

## Materials

Bubble pack sheets
Different colors of
fingerpaint
Spoons
Variety of surfaces:
> Tabletop
> Placemats
> Fingerpaint paper
> Large plastic trays
> Freezer wrap paper
> Cookie sheets
> Carpet protectors
> Rubber bath mats
> Linoleum

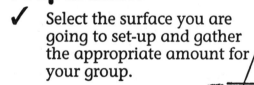

## Preparation

✓ Select the surface you are
going to set-up and gather
the appropriate amount for
your group.

## Activity

Put the fingerpaint and spoons on the art table along with the sheets of
bubble pack. As the children want to fingerpaint, have them spoon paint
onto the bubble pack and then paint with their fingers, knuckles, palms, and
nails.

***EXTENSION:*** *Using large sheets of paper make prints of the children's
fingerpaintings. Let them dry and then hang them around the room.*

***VARIATION:*** *Offer fingerpainting often, varying the surfaces and colors of paint.*

# Buddy Painting

## Materials

Packing foam
Forks
Pie pans/meat trays
Tempera paint
Appliance box

## Preparation

✓ Make Foam Daubers:

    **1.** Cut the packing foam into 2"x3" pieces.

    **2.** Poke a fork into each piece for a handle.

✓ Pour a shallow amount of the tempera paint into pie pans.

✓ Put 1 or 2 foam daubers on each paint tray.

## Activity

Put newspaper or a large piece of plastic on the floor in the art area. Set the appliance box on top. Place the paint trays and foam daubers on the floor around the box.

Have the children paint the appliance box. Let it dry overnight. During the next day talk with the children about how they would like to use the box in the classroom. To begin the discussion suggest a room decoration, a quiet place to read, a puppet stage, a tent for outside, and so on.

# Colored Sand Painting

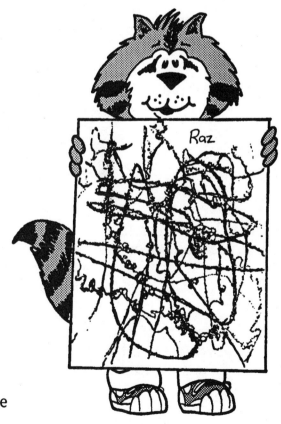

## Materials

Sand
Sturdy paper plates/pie pans
Colored chalk
Unbreakable salt shakers/small containers
White glue in squeeze bottles
Food coloring
Construction paper

## Preparation

✓ Pour sand on the paper plates/pie pans

✓ Put one color of chalk on each plate/pie pan.

✓ Mix the food coloring into your white glue to make it colored and then pour it back into the squeeze bottles.

## Activity

This is a two part activity.

**1.** Color the sand. Put the pie pans of sand on the table. Have the children rub the sand with chalk to color it. After each pan of sand has been colored, use a funnel and pour the sand into a small container or salt shaker.

**2.** Put the colored glue, sand, and paper on the table. Let the children drizzle a glue design on their paper and then sprinkle the sand over the design by shaking it from the salt shakers or picking it up with their fingers and slowly dropping it along the glue line.

Let the Sand Paintings dry and then shake off the excess sand into a large container.

# Comb Painting

## Materials

Different combs

Squeeze bottles (like ketchup/mustard)

Tempera paint

Flour

Dish tub

Light colored shelf paper

## Preparation

✓ Thicken your tempera paint: (You may prefer to do this with the children.)

1. Pour one color paint into a large bowl.

2. Slowly add flour to the paint, stirring all the while.

Continue thickening the paint until it is about the consistency of thick ketchup. If it gets too thick, simply add more paint and stir.

✓ Pour the thickened paint into squeeze bottles.

✓ Pour water into a dish tub.

## Activity

Put the squeeze bottles, combs, and dish tub on the art table. Have the roll of shelf paper and scissors nearby. As each child is ready to paint, have her decide how long a sheet of paper she'd like. She can cut it off the roll and lay it on the table. You may need to tape the shelf paper down to prevent it from curling up.

Let her squeeze as many different colors of paint on her paper as she would like and then take the combs and begin 'running' them through the colors. As she is 'Comb Painting' she may want to add more paint or try different combs.

When finished have her rinse her combs in the tub of water so they are clean for other painters.

# Construction Paper Collage Painting

## Materials

Different colors of crepe and/or construction paper

Spray bottles

White paper

## Preparation

✓  Pour water into several spray bottles.

✓  Put scraps of different colored construction paper/crepe paper on meat trays.

## Activity

Put the spray bottles and scraps of paper on the art table. Have the white paper nearby. Lay some newspaper on the floor in a secluded area.

Have the children lay their paper on the art table and then spray it with water. After the paper is wet, take pieces of colored paper and tear them up. Set the pieces on the wet paper, and press them down so they 'stick' to the paper. When a child finishes her paper collage, have her set it on the newspaper to dry. After it is dry encourage the child to pick up the colored paper and look at her painting.

**VARIATION:** *Fill a large dish tub about 1/3 full of water. Instead of spraying the paper to get it wet, dip the paper into the tub of water, let it sit for several seconds, and then pull it out. Once wet the children can continue the activity as above.*

# Cookie Cutter Printing

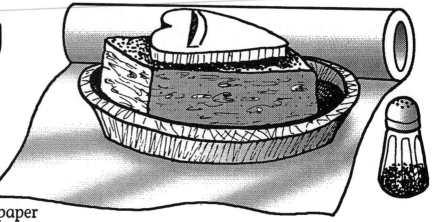

## Materials

Giant sponges
Cookie cutters
Pie pans
Dry tempera paint
Wide plain color shelf paper

## Preparation

✓ Put different colors of dry tempera paint in salt shakers. Set one wet sponge in each pie pan. Add a little water to each pan so that the sponges stay moist.

✓ Cut a piece of shelf paper the length of your art table.

## Activity

Lay the shelf paper on your art table/floor. Put the sponges and cookie cutters around the edges of the paper. Let the children shake dry tempera paint on each sponge. When finished put the salt shaker in the pie pan.

Have the children press the cookie cutters onto the sponges and then print on the shelf paper. When the color becomes weak, simply shake more dry tempera on the sponges. Keep printing until the paper is filled with different colored prints.

# Cookie Painting

## Materials

Graham crackers
Cotton swabs
Small bowls or
empty tuna cans
Light Karo® syrup
Water
Food coloring

## Preparation

✓ Mix the 'Cookie Paint.' For each color: (You may prefer to mix the 'cookie paint' with the children.)
  1. Measure 1 teaspoon of Karo® syrup and put it in a small bowl.
  2. Add 1/4t of water and using a fork mix with the syrup.
  3. Add a drop of food coloring and mix again.
  4. Repeat the process for each color of 'Cookie Paint' you want.

✓ Put cotton swabs on a small tray.

## Activity

Put several plates of graham crackers, cotton swabs, and the bowls of 'Cookie Paint' on the table. Have a large tray or cookie sheet at one end. Let the children 'paint' the graham crackers with the different colors. As they finish each one have them gently set it on the tray. Enjoy the specially painted treat for snack or dessert with milk or juice.

**HINT:** *Change the cotton swabs often so that you don't get threads of cotton on your crackers.*

**VARIATION:** *Instead of painting graham crackers, paint unsweetened vanilla cookies or other types of crackers.*

# Cornstarch Goo Fingerpainting

## Materials

Cornstarch
Water
Food coloring
Large unbreakable trays
Non-sensitive skin lotion (optional)

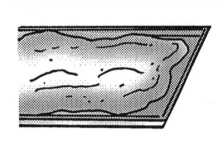

## Preparation

✓ Mix the 'Cornstarch Goo'. You could do this with the children. For each color:

1. Pour 2 cups of cornstarch into a large bowl.

2. Pour 1 1/2 cups of water into the bowl.

3. Slowly stir the ingredients together. When it is partially mixed, add a few drops of food coloring and continue to stir.

4. When mixed, pour the Goo on a large tray. Cover the mixture with a damp cloth until the children are ready to use it.

5. Repeat for each color you want.

## Activity

Put the trays of Cornstarch Goo on the art table. Let the children 'dig' their fingertips into the mixture and begin fingerpainting. Encourage the children to use their knuckles, palms, and whole hands. Talk about how the Goo feels and looks. Is it like other fingerpaint? Different?

When each child is finished, have her wash and then put a little lotion on her hands. The cornstarch is drying to the skin and the lotion feels good.

**VARIATION:** *Instead of mixing cornstarch and water mix equal amounts of salt, flour and water. Add color if you want. Compare the two fingerpaints.*

# Cotton Dauber Painting

## Materials

Cotton batting
Chip clips/clothespins
Dry tempera
Containers such as margarine tubs
Several spray bottles
Trays
Paper towels
White paper

## Preparation

 Make Cotton Daubers:
1. Pull wads of cotton off of the big piece.
2. Clip a 'chip clip' or clothespin to each one for a handle.

✓ Pour different colors of dry tempera paint into the containers.

✓ Pour water into your spray bottles.

## Activity

Set the cotton daubers, containers of dry tempera paint, and spray bottles on your art table. Have the paper, trays, and paper towels nearby.

Have your children put pieces of paper on their trays and set them on the table. Let the children use the cotton daubers to smear the colors of dry tempera all over their papers. Then let them lightly spray their papers with water. (Watch the paint.) Set the paintings off to the side to dry. If necessary, use a sponge or paper towel to dry off the tray so that it is ready for another child when he wants to paint.

# Crayon Painting

## Materials

Old crayons
Warming tray
Aluminum foil
Meat tray
Wooden block (optional)

## Preparation

✓ Have the children help you peel the paper off of the old crayons.

✓ Put them on a meat tray or pie pan.

✓ Put the warming tray on a table in a quiet area of the room. Tape the cord to the floor for safety.

## Activity

Put the aluminum foil and crayons near the warming tray. Turn the tray on warm or low. When a child wants to Crayon Paint have him tear a piece of aluminum foil, set it on the tray, and very slowly move the crayons across the foil to create a picture or design. Continue for as long as he would like.

### HINTS:

■ *Push the warming tray away from the edge of the table so children do not lean on it.*

■ *Have the children hold the crayons at the top so their hands/fingers do not touch the warming tray.*

■ *Have children rest the arm that's holding the aluminum foil on the wooden block.*

■ *Because this is an individual activity have a clipboard with paper and pencil. Have children 'sign-up' if they want to do the activity. As each child is finished, have her cross her name off of the list and ask the next child if he is ready to paint. Remember, they can sign-up as often as they'd like or change their minds when it is their turn.*

# Dancing Fingers Fingerpainting

## Materials

Record player
Favorite dancing/marching music
Small containers
Small spoons
Fingerpaint
Paper towels
Butcher paper

## Preparation

✓ Put different colors of fingerpaint into small containers.

✓ Put a small spoon in each container.

✓ Cut the butcher paper long enough for children to sit around and fingerpaint.

## Activity

This is a small or large group activity. Spread out the sheet of butcher paper in an open area of the classroom. Set the containers of paint around the paper.

Have the children sit around the paper and each scoop fingerpaint onto the space in front of him. When everyone is ready, begin playing the music. Encourage the children to dance their fingers as they listen to the music and fingerpaint. After awhile stop the music, let the children add more paint, and then dance some more. Continue dancing until the paper is filled with all colors and designs of fingerpaint. Afterwards let the children wipe their hands with paper towels.

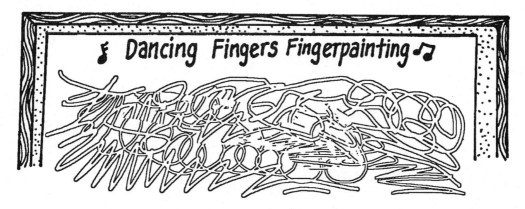

# Dauber Printing

## Materials

Muslin fabric
Polyfil
Tempera paint
Small meat trays
Paper lunch bags
Newspaper
Yarn

## Preparation

✓ Pour shallow amounts of different colors of tempera paint onto small meat trays.

✓ Make your daubers:

1. Cut your muslin into 4" squares.

2. Put a little polyfil into the middle of each square.

3. Gather up the corners of the muslin and fasten each one closed with a rubber band.

4. Put one or two daubers on each meat tray.

## Activity

Have the paper bags, paint trays, and daubers on the art table. Let each child daub paint on his bag anyway he chooses. Some children may choose to daub a face, others a pre-determined design, and still others will simply daub randomly. Let the paint dry.

**EXTENSION:** *After the paint has dried, have the children open their bags and stuff them with wads of newspaper. Use the yarn to tie each child's bag closed.*

# Drip-Drop Painting

## Materials

Small aluminum foil pie pans
Tempera paint
Small pitchers
Butcher paper

## Preparation

✓ Fill each pitcher about 1/4 full of a different color of tempera paint.
✓ Add water to each pitcher and mix so that the paint is fairly thin.
✓ Poke several small holes in each aluminum foil pan.
✓ Cut your butcher paper the length of your art table.

## Activity

Lay the butcher paper on your art table/floor. Set the aluminum foil pans and pitchers of paint around the edges.

Have the children paint in pairs. One child holds the pie pan over the paper and her partner slowly pours a little paint into the pie pan. Slowly rock the pie pan back and forth and watch the paint drip onto the paper. Pour more paint into the pie pans and drip more colorful drops. Continue Drip-Drop Painting using the same and different colors.

As the Drip-Drop Painting develops watch the shapes of the drips and the new colors as the paints mix together.

# Drip Painting

## Materials

Children's socks
Thick sponges
Tempera paint
Pie pans
Large appliance box
Newspapers

## Preparation

✓ Cut the sides off of the appliance box.

✓ Water down your paint a little. Pour shallow amounts of each color into a pie pan.

✓ Make your Daubers:
  1. Cut your sponge/s into fairly large pieces which fit into the children's socks.
  2. Put one sponge in the toe of each sock.
  3. Tie the tops of the socks closed with rubber bands or pieces of yarn/heavy string.
  4. Put several daubers in each pie pan.

   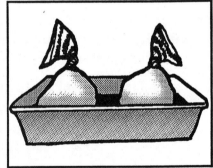

## Activity

Lean one or two sides of your appliance box against an empty wall. Lay newspaper on the floor along the bottom edge. Set your pie pans of paint on the newspaper.

Have children choose one or two daubers, wiggle them in the paint and then press them against the cardboard. Watch the paint drip. Re-dip the daubers or change colors and press again and again.

## Display

After your Drip Painting has dried hang it on a wall in your block area.

# Drizzle Painting

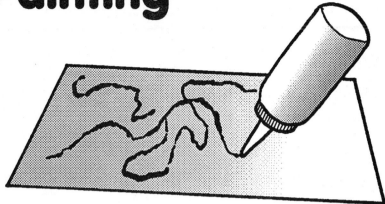

## Materials

White glue
Small squeeze bottles
Food coloring
Small bowls
Construction paper

## Preparation

✓ Pour white glue into one of the small bowls. Mix in a little water so that it becomes slightly more liquid. Add several drops of food coloring to the glue and stir until thoroughly blended. Add more coloring if necessary. Repeat for each color.

✓ Pour each color of glue into a squeeze bottle.

## Activity

Put the squeeze bottles on the art table. Have the construction paper nearby. As each child chooses to Drizzle Paint, have her select a piece of construction paper and lay it on the table. Let her squeeze the bottles and drizzle thin and thick lines of color all over her paper.

*VARIATION: When blending the glue, water, and food coloring, add glitter to the mixture. Now offer the activity using all glittered glue. Another time use glittered and unglittered glue.*

# Drop Painting

## Materials

Wide-mouthed plastic straws
Small containers
Tempera paint
Construction paper

## Preparation

✓ Water down your paint so that it is fairly thin.
Fill each container about halfway up.

✓ Cut your straws in half.

## Activity

Set the containers of paint on the table. Put several straws in each container.

Show the children how to 'catch the paint' by putting their straws in the paint, covering the tops of the straws with their index fingers, and slowly lifting them out of the paint. Move the paint-filled straws over the construction paper, lift their fingers off the tops of the straws, and watch the paint drop.

Encourage the children to hold their straws at different heights. Continue with lots of the same and different colored drops.

*VARIATION: Fill your containers with a little paint. Give each child her own straw. Have her 'capture the paint' as explained above, but this time have her blow the paint out of the straw rather than let it drip. When she is finished painting, remind her to throw her straw away.*

# Eraser Printing

## Materials

Shaped erasers, such as dinosaurs
Small meat trays
Paper towels
Tempera paint
Construction paper

## Preparation

✓ Cut some of your construction paper in half.

✓ Make different colored printing pads. To make each pad:

1. Fold several paper towels together so that they form a thick pad which fits on a meat tray.

2. Set the paper towel pad on the meat tray. Slowly pour paint over the pad.

3. Roll the paint into the towel with a brayer or wallpaper seam roller. You want your pad to be moist, but not too soggy.

4. Repeat the process for each printing pad.

✓ If you do not have shape erasers, cut your own. You'll need large gum erasers, miniature cookie cutters, and a paring knife.

To make each shape eraser:

1. Draw a simple shape on the eraser with a ball point pen or press a cookie cutter into it.

2. Using your knife carefully cut the eraser away from the shape so that the shape is raised about 1/4". (Remember safety.)

3. Repeat for each shape.

## Activity

Set full and half-size sheets of construction paper, printing pads, and eraser shapes on the art table. Have the children choose what size paper they want to use. Let the children print all different shapes and colors.

**EXTENSION:** *If a child wants to tell a story about the prints, you could write what he says on another sheet of paper and staple it to the 'printed' page.*

# Eyedropper Painting

## Materials

Wide adding machine tape

Removable adhesive tape

Unbreakable eyedroppers

Food coloring

Paper punches

Construction paper

## Preparation

✓ Mix food coloring and water or water-down your tempera paint until it is very thin. Pour the colors in small containers.

✓ Put at least one eyedropper in each container.

## Activity

Put the containers of paint on the art table. Have each child show you how long a strip of adding machine tape she'd like. Cut it for her or let her do it herself. Let her punch as many holes in her strip as she'd like.

After she's finished 'punching' holes, fasten the strip to a piece of construction paper. Using the eyedroppers, let her drop colors of paint into the holes. Let the paint dry. Carefully lift the strip up and refasten it to an empty space on the construction paper. Repeat as often as she would like.

**VARIATION:** *Cut a big square of butcher paper and different length strips of adding machine tape. Let the children punch holes in each strip. As each strip is finished, tape it to the butcher paper. Put the big square on the art table along with the paint containers and eyedroppers. Have the children drop dots of color in all of the holes. Let the paint dry, lift up the strips, and hang the Polka Dot Painting on an empty wall.*

# Face Painting

## Materials

4T shortening
10T cornstarch
2T flour
1/4t glycerin
Food coloring
Small bowls

> # Note: To remove the face paint—put cold cream, shortening, or baby oil on a tissue and gently rub off your child's face paint.

## Preparation

✓ Mix the Face Paint:
   **1.** Using a rubber spatula, blend the first three ingredients.
   **2.** Add glycerin and mix again.
   **3.** Divide the mixture into as many smaller portions as you want colors. Put each portion in a small unbreakable bowl.
   **4.** Mix a little food coloring into each bowl.

## Activity

Set up a special 'Face Painting' area. Have a table, several chairs, and a full length mirror as well as several unbreakable hand-held mirrors.

Let the children make up their own faces or if more appropriate for your children, ask a volunteer to do it with each child.

**HINT:** *Send a special note home to families telling them which day you will be face painting and how to remove the paint — "Put cold cream, shortening, or baby oil on a tissue and gently rub off the paint."*

# Fingerpainting At The Easel

## Materials

Tempera paint/fingerpaint
Evaporated milk
Small containers such as tuna cans
Fingerpaint paper/freezer wrap paper
Small spray bottle

## Preparation

✓ Fill the spray bottle about half full of water.

✓ Mix a little evaporated milk with each color of paint to make it glossy.

✓ Pour each color into a small container.

✓ If necessary cut your paper the size of your easel.

## Activity

Put the paint in your easel trays. Set the small water bottle near the easel. Have each child clip a piece of paper to the easel and then spray his paper with water. (Have him count "1,2" as he pumps the spray bottle.) Encourage him to fingerpaint as long as he wants, using as many different colors as he would like.

**HINT:** *If the paper gets too dry, have him spray it with "one" pump and then continue to paint.*

# Flick Finger Painting

## Materials

Watercolor markers
Several small containers
White paper

## Preparation

✓ Pour shallow amounts
of water into the
small containers.

## Activity

Put the watercolor markers and containers of water on the art table. Have the white paper nearby.

Have the children use the watercolor markers to draw a picture, design, or scribble. When they are finished, let them dip their fingers in the water and 'flick' the water on their drawings. What happens? Let children continue to 'flick' as much water on their drawings as they'd like. When finished have each child carefully move his painting to a secluded place to dry.

# Fly Swatter Printing

## Materials

Clean fly swatters
Pie pans
Tempera paint
Butcher paper

## Preparation

✓ Pour shallow amounts of different colors of paint into pie pans.

✓ Cut a long piece of butcher paper and roll it up to take outside.

## Activity

Roll the piece of butcher paper out in a secluded area of the playground. Put a brick on each corner of the paper to hold it down. Set the pie pans of paint around the edges of the paper. Set a fly swatter in each one.

Let the children lift the fly swatters out of the paint and slap them on the paint. Slap again and again until the print becomes weak. Lay the fly swatters in the paint again and print some more.

Leave the activity set-up while you are outside. When it is time to go inside, leave the mural there to dry. After dry, gently bring it inside and hang it low on a wall for everyone to look at. If weather permits, you might want to hang it on your outside fence.

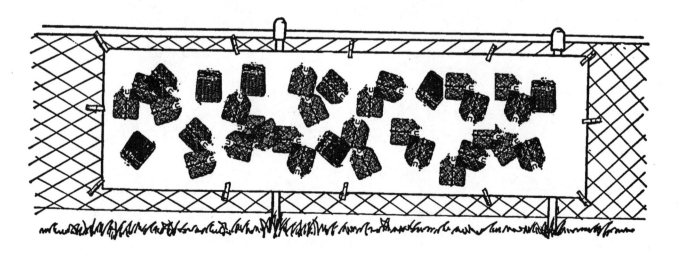

# Fold-Overs

## Materials

Soft perm bottles
Tempera paint
Light colored paper

## Preparation

✓ Snip the very tip of each perm bottle so that there is a small hole in each one.
✓ Pour a different color of tempera paint into each bottle.
✓ Fold each piece of paper in half.

## Activity

Set the paper and the perm bottles of paint on the art table. Have children (or you) write their names on one half of the paper. Encourage each child to use the different colors of paint to create a design of squiggles, lines, dots, curves, and puddles on the half of his paper with his name.

After he's finished creating his design, have him fold the blank side of his paper over his design. Very slowly rub the top of the folded-over paper. Keep rubbing! After rubbing the entire paper, carefully open it up. What do you see?

**VARIATION:** *If you have younger children, let them create designs on unfolded paper. After each child has finished, let him lay a blank piece of paper over his design. Now have him slowly and gently rub the entire paper. Separate the two pages. Do they look similar?*

**HINT:** *You need to rub longer and slower than you might imagine to get a good print.*

# Food Baster Painting

## Materials

Food Basters
Small Pails
Food coloring

## Preparation

✓ Mix food coloring and water to make brilliant colors. Pour the different colors in the pails.

✓ Put all of the basters in a separate pail.

## Activity

On a day when the ground is full of snow, have the children help you carry the 'pails of paint' and the basters outside. Set the pails in the snow. Let the children help you put at least one baster in each color.

During the time they are playing outside, let them 'paint' the snow. Depending on your space they can 'paint' all of the snow or confine their 'painting' to a specific area. To 'paint' have the children suck paint into the basters and then drip it over the snow. Refill the basters and squirt some more.

# Frozen Color Painting

## Materials

Popsicle sticks/plastic forks
Small disposable cups
Tempera paint
Small meat trays
Butcher paper

## Preparation

✓ Make large colored ice cubes:

**1.** Fill the cups 3/4 full of water. Add a different color of tempera paint to each cup. Stir the paint into the water until it is thoroughly mixed.

**2.** Put the cups in the freezer. When the molds are partially hardened, put a popsicle stick or plastic fork in each one.

✓ Cut the butcher paper the length of your art table.

## Activity

Lay the butcher paper on the art table/floor. Just before the activity, take the ice cubes out of the freezer. Let the children help you peel the cups away from the ice. Put each cube on a small meat tray. Set the trays around the paper.

Let the children use one or two cubes at a time and smear color all over the paper.

# Giant Blob-Oh Printing

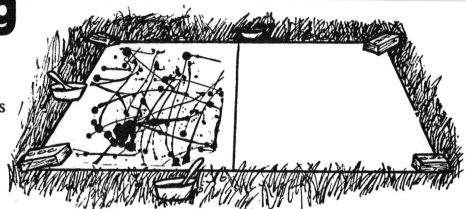

## Materials

Margarine containers with covers
Sturdy small spoons
Tempera paint
Butcher paper

## Preparation

✓ Pour different colors of paint into margarine containers. Cover them.

✓ Cut a long sheet of butcher paper and roll it up to take outside.

## Activity

Carry the paint, butcher paper, and spoons outside. Lay the paper in a quiet area of the playground. Secure each corner with a brick or rock. Using a wide marker draw a vertical line down the middle of the paper. Put the margarine tubs and spoons around one end of the paper.

Have the children fill their spoons with paint and 'flick' them at that end of the paper. Keep 'flicking' paint until the paper is filled with all colors of blobs.

Carefully fold the blank half over the painted half. Have several children at a time take off their shoes and socks and walk on the Giant Blob-Oh to make the print. After everyone has walked on the art, gently open it up and look at your new painting.

# Glove Fingerpainting

## Materials

Small containers
Small spoons
Fingerpaint
Different pairs of old gloves:
> *Rubber gloves*
> *Garden gloves*
> *Leather gloves*
> *Dress gloves*
> *Winter-type gloves*
> *Surgical gloves*
> *Work gloves*

## Preparation

✓ Put different colors of fingerpaint into small containers.

✓ Add a spoon to each container.

✓ Put the gloves in a box.

## Activity

Put the box of gloves and the containers of fingerpaint on the art table. When the children come to fingerpaint, have them put on gloves, spoon paint onto the table, and fingerpaint with the gloves on.

**HINT:** *Children might want to paint with one gloved and one ungloved hand, two different gloves, or a matching pair of gloves.*

# Glue Glob Painting

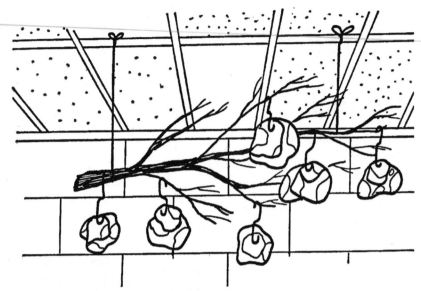

## Materials

White glue
Watercolor paint
Small squeeze bottles
Small containers like margarine tubs
Paper towels
Waxed paper

## Preparation

✓ Water-down your white glue so that it easily squeezes out of the glue bottles. (Only if your glue is thick.)

✓ Pour the glue into small squeeze type bottles.

✓ Pour water into several small containers like margarine tubs.

## Activity

This is a 2 day activity.

**Day 1** - Put the glue bottles on the table. Help each child tear a small piece of waxed paper to work on. Let her drizzle globs of glue on it. After she's drizzled her Glue Glob, have her put it in a quiet place to dry. When it has almost hardened, put a paper clip hanger on it.

**Day 2** - Let her paint her Glue Glob design by dipping her pointer finger into the water, squiggling it in a watercolor paint, and then using her finger to paint her 'globs'. Continue painting with the same or different colors. When each child is finished have her set her colorful Glue Glob off to the side to dry. Hang the Glue Globs on an inside tree branch.

*HINT:* In between colors encourage her to dry her 'painting finger' on the paper towels. This will keep the watercolors more brilliant.

*VARIATION:* Use colored water and unbreakable eyedroppers instead of watercolors and fingers.

# Golf Ball Buddy Painting

## Materials

Large heavy-duty box/es
Golf balls
Medium size containers
Tempera paint
Spoons
Butcher paper

## Preparation

✓ Pour different colors of paint in the medium containers.

✓ Put several golf balls and a spoon in each container.

✓ Cut the butcher paper to fit in the box/es.

## Activity

Set the large boxes, paint containers, and paper on the art table. When pairs of children come to art, have them lay a piece of paper in the box and then spoon several paint-filled golf balls into the box. Each child should pick up one end of the box and together begin rolling the golf balls around. When the paint is off the golf balls the children can re-dip the balls and paint some more or lay it down to dry.

# Gym Shoe Printing

## Materials

7-8 pairs of different
types/sizes of gym shoes
Tempera paint
Brownie pans
Butcher paper
Newspaper

## Preparation

✓ Cut the butcher paper the length of your art table.

✓ Pour shallow amounts of different colors of tempera paint into the brownie pans. (Refill as necessary while the children are printing.)

✓ Put newspaper on the floor near the art table.

## Activity

Lay the butcher paper on your art table/floor. Set the pans of paint around the edges of the paper. Have the shoes on the floor near the activity.

Have a child pick a pair of gym shoes and slip one shoe on each hand. (You might talk with him about who might really wear these shoes. How does he know?) Put the shoes in the paint and wiggle them around to get the bottoms full of color. Carefully lift the shoes out of the paint and begin 'walking' along the paper. Encourage each child to watch his trail as he walks along. If he re-dips his shoes he may want to use a different color.

After his 'walk' have the child slip the shoes off of his hands and put them on the newspaper. After everyone has taken a walk, let the mural dry, and then hang it up.

# Handprints At The Easel

## Materials

2 small tables
Pie pans
Tempera paint
Paper towels
Easel paper

## Preparation

✓ Put a small table on each side of your easel.
✓ Pour shallow amounts of different colors of paint into the pie pans.
✓ Tear paper towels into separate sheets.

## Activity

Put the paper towels and several pie pans of paint on each table next to your easel. Have plenty of easel paper handy for the children to use.

Have the children push up their sleeves, press their hands into the paint, and then print their handprints on the easel paper. Do again and again using different colors of paint and/or printing their hands in different positions.

When finished let them wipe the excess paint off of their hands with a paper towel.

*VARIATION: Let two children 'buddy paint' by making handprints together on the same piece of easel paper.*

# Hands Around The Room

## Materials

Large meat trays
Paper towels
Tempera paint
Narrow plain color shelf paper

## Preparation

✓ Cut the shelf paper into 5 foot lengths.

✓ Make different colored printing pads. To make each pad:

   **1.** Lay a stack of paper towels together so that they form a thick pad which fits on a meat tray.

   **2.** Set the paper towel pad on the meat tray. Slowly pour one color of paint over the pad. Let the paint soak in. The pad should be fairly moist. Pour more paint if necessary.

   **3.** Repeat the process for each printing pad.

## Activity

Lay one length of shelf paper on the floor/table. Set the paint around the edges. Have children press their hands onto the paint pad and then print a set of hand prints on the paper. Write the child's name near her prints. When one paper is full of prints, lay down another strip and continue. Keep printing until all of the children have made as many sets of hand prints as they want.

## Display

*Hang the hands all around the room — near the ceiling, along the baseboard, or at the children's eye level.*

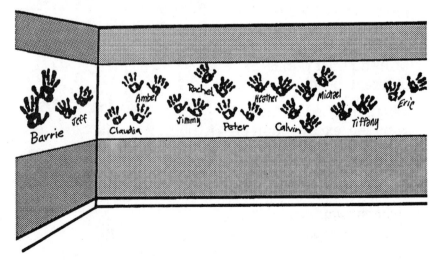

# Ice Cube Painting

## Materials

Mittens
Ice cubes
Dry tempera
Unbreakable salt shakers
Paper plates

## Preparation

✓ Make lots of ice cubes and put them in an ice chest.

✓ Pour dry tempera paint into salt shakers.

## Activity

Set the mittens, ice cubes, and salt shakers filled with dry paint on the table. Have the paper plates nearby.

Let children take plates and sprinkle all colors of dry tempera on them. Then put on mittens, pick up one or two ice cubes, and slowly move them through the paint.

When each child is finished have her put the ice cubes back and set her plate in a secluded area to dry.

# Ice Mold Painting

## Materials

Variety of small containers:
- *Cups*
- *Muffin tins*
- *Margarine tubs*
- *Small pie pans*
- *Gelatin molds*

Small aluminum pie pans
Tempera paint
Several pairs of tongs
Coffee stir sticks
Unbreakable eyedroppers
Construction paper

## Preparation

✓ Fill each container with water and freeze. Be sure to make enough molds for all of the children.

✓ Put the stir sticks in a separate cup.

✓ Pour the tempera paint into small containers.

✓ Have an aluminum pie pan or other non-paper container for each child.

## Activity

On the day of the activity, pop out the different ice molds and store them in an ice chest. Set the ice chest near the art table. Put the paint, stir sticks, and small containers on the table.

Let each child choose her own ice mold from the chest, pick it up with the tongs, and set it in a small container. (Write the child's name on a piece of masking tape and stick it to the container.) Then, dip the stir sticks in paint, pull them out, and drip paint onto the ice mold. Let each child drip as much paint as she would like.

After each child has finished painting her mold, have her carefully set it off to the side. Encourage the children to watch their molds melt. Maybe some children will want to drip even more paint on the mold.

When the child's mold has totally melted, let her mix her paint and water and then use eyedroppers and the watercolor paint she has made to create a Dot Painting on construction paper.

# Icicle Painting

## Materials

Icicle/s from around your building

Large tray
Mittens
Tempera paint cakes
Butcher paper

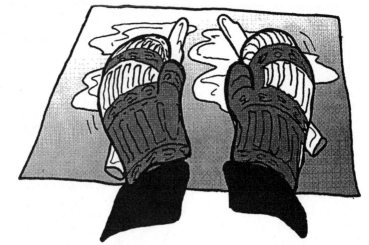

## Preparation

✓ Break off several icicles hanging from your roof. If there are sharp points, break them off. Put the icicles on a tray. (You may prefer to take a walk with the children and let them choose what icicles to break off.)

✓ Put each tempera paint cake on a small meat tray.

✓ Cut a piece of butcher paper the length of your art table.

## Activity

Lay the piece of butcher paper on the art table/floor. Set the trays of paint, mittens, and icicles around the edges of the paper.

Have the children put mittens on and then wet-down sections of the butcher paper by smearing them with icicles. When a child's section is wet, let him use the paint cakes to smear a design. If the section gets too dry, use the icicle to wet it down again. Let children continue until the mural is full of color.

**VARIATION:** *Instead of using tempera paint cakes, the children could shake dry tempera paint on the wet paper.*

# Leaf Printing

## Materials

Leaves
Meat trays
Paper towels
Tempera paint
Brayers/wallpaper
seam rollers
Muslin/plain fabric
White paper

## Preparation

✓ Cut your fabric into small pieces (6"x12" or 6"x15") so that children can easily print leaves on each one.

✓ Collect a wide variety of leaves. You may want to take the children on a 'leaf hunt' and let them collect the leaves for the activity.

✓ Put the leaves on a tray.

✓ Cut the white paper in half.

✓ Make different colored printing pads. To make each pad:
1. Fold several paper towels together so that they form a thick pad which fits on a meat tray.

2. Set the paper towel pad on the meat tray. Pour the paint onto the towel.

3. Roll the paint into the pad with a roller. You want your pad to be moist but not soggy.

4. Repeat the process for each printing pad.

## Activity

Set the fabric pieces, rollers, white paper, printing pads, and tray of leaves on the art table.

When a child wants to Leaf Print have her put a piece of fabric in front of her and then choose a leaf from the tray. Have her lay it, bottom-side down, on one of the printing pads. Use a roller to slowly roll the leaf into the paint. Pick up the painted leaf, lay it on the fabric, cover it with a piece of white paper, and slowly, with a little pressure, roll it again. Lift off the white paper, pick up the leaf, and look at your print. Make more leaf prints with other leaves or the same one.

**HINT:** *Add more paint to the printing pads as necessary.*

# Lid Printing

## Materials

Round jar lids and caps
Meat trays
Tempera paint
Butcher paper

## Preparation

✓ Collect a wide variety of round jar lids and caps.

✓ Pour shallow amounts of different colors of paint onto meat trays. Set several lids/caps in the paint.

✓ Cut the paper into as large a circle as possible.

## Activity

Lay the piece of paper on the floor/art table. Put the paint trays with the lids and caps around the circle. Encourage the children to paint with different colors of paint and sizes of circles.

**EXTENSION:** *On a different day cut a giant rectangle out of butcher paper or newsprint. Collect various sizes of box tops and let the children print with these. Repeat with square and triangle shapes or a potpourri of all shapes.*

# Making Tracks Painting

## Materials

Shaving cream
Track makers:
> Corks
> Cups
> Tongue depressors
> Popsicle sticks

## Preparation

✓ None

## Activity

Spray shaving cream on the art table. Have several trays of 'Track Makers' around the edges of the table.

Let children enjoy fingerpainting in the shaving cream. In addition encourage them to smear the shaving cream around the table and make tracks using the various track makers.

# Marble Painting

## Materials

Marbles
Margarine tubs
Cylindrical containers such as
oatmeal, chips, corn meal, coffee
Spoons
Tempera paint
White duplicating paper

## Preparation

✓ Pour different colors of paint
   into the tubs.
✓ Put several marbles into each tub.
✓ Put a spoon in each tub.

## Activity

Put the cylindrical containers,
paper and tubs of paint on
the art table. When a child comes
to the activity have him roll
up a piece of paper and put it in a
cylinder. Roll the marbles
around in the paint and spoon
them into the cylinder. Put the
top on the container and begin to
shake, roll, and tip it back and
forth. After awhile, dump the
marbles back into the paint tubs,
roll them around again, put them
back in the cylinder, and shake
some more. Continue for as long
as the child would like. When he
is finished, have him take his
painting out of the cylinder, let it
dry, and then hang it up.

# Marbleized Painting

## Materials

Large, shallow container
Several small pitchers
Several colors of oil-based paint
Several popsicle sticks
Newspaper
Clothesline
Clothespins
White construction paper

## Preparation

✓ Fill the pitchers about half full of water.

✓ String the clothesline near the art table and lay newspapers on the floor under it.

## Activity

Set the pitchers of water, large container, popsicle sticks, clothespins, and paint on the art table. Have the paper nearby.

Have a child pour water into the large container so that is about half to three-quarters full. Next let several children dribble a little paint onto the water. (It will float.) Let a child swirl the colors around and around. Then clip a clothespin to the paper and slowly dip the paper in and out of the water. Hang the painting on the clothesline to dry. When another child wants to paint, let him swirl the water again and paint.

**HINT:** *Oil-based paint dries slowly and thus should be left hanging overnight.*

# Masher Printing

## Materials

Variety of potato mashers
Spring whisks
4-5 colors of tempera paint
Solid color old sheet

## Preparation

✓ Lay the bedsheet on the floor. Using a fabric marker divide the sheet into as many sections as you have children.

✓ Pour shallow amounts of different colors of paint into pie pans.

## Activity

Lay the bedsheet on the floor/table in your art area. Set the pie pans, potato mashers, and spring whisks around the edges of the sheet if it is on the floor, or the edges of the table if it is on the art table.

Let each child choose a section of the sheet. You write the child's name in the section. Let the children dip utensils into the paint and print in their sections on the sheet. Continue with all of the different utensils and colors. You might leave this activity out for several days.

**VARIATION:** *Instead of sectioning off the sheet, let each child simply print on the sheet. When each is finished, write his/her name near the prints.*

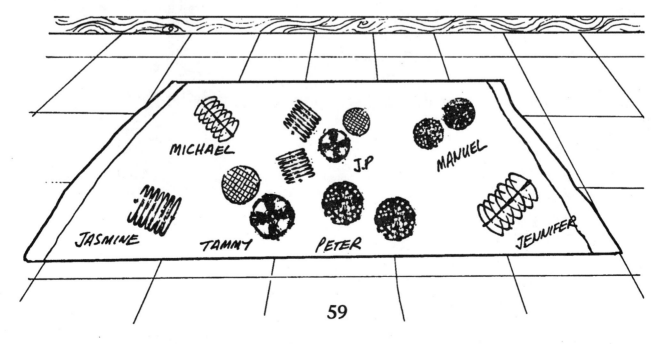

59

# Melted Crayon Painting

## Materials

Old crayons
Aluminum foil cupcake containers
Cotton swabs/coffee stir sticks
Styrofoam meat trays
Paper clips

## Preparation

✓ Have the children help you peel the paper off of the old crayons.

✓ Break the crayons into small pieces.

✓ Put each color of crayon into a separate cupcake container.

✓ Set all of the containers on a tray.

✓ Cut the meat trays into small recognizable and/or free-form shapes.

## Activity

Do this activity inside or outside.

On a warm sunny day put the tray of old crayon pieces outside. Watch the crayons melt. After they have melted, put the styrofoam shapes, cotton swabs, and 'crayon paint' on the table. Let the children paint one or both sides of their styrofoam pieces.

When each child is finished help him hook a paper clip hanger to his art and then hang it on a large tree branch.

# Newspaper Printing

## Materials

Newspaper
Tempera paint
Meat trays
Old bedsheet

## Preparation

✓  Cut the newspaper into half-size pieces and set them into several boxes.

✓  Pour shallow amounts of different colors of tempera paint onto the meat trays.

## Activity

Lay the bedsheet inside on the art table or outside on the grass. Set the trays of paint and boxes of newspaper around the sheet. Have the children wad up pieces of newspaper, dip them in the paint, and print all over the sheet.

Let the paint dry and then hang in a prominent place for everyone to see.

# Paint And Print Fingerpainting

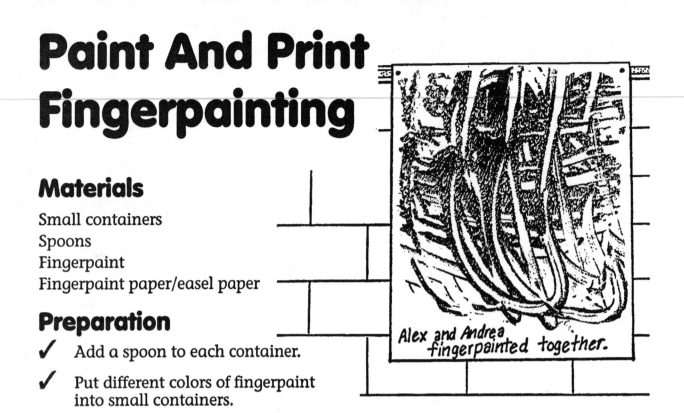

Alex and Andrea fingerpainted together.

## Materials

Small containers
Spoons
Fingerpaint
Fingerpaint paper/easel paper

## Preparation

✓ Add a spoon to each container.

✓ Put different colors of fingerpaint into small containers.

## Activity

Put the fingerpaint on the art table. When the children come to paint, let them spoon paint on the table and fingerpaint right on the tabletop.

When each child is finished fingerpainting, ask her if she would like you to make a print of her fingerpaint design. If so, carefully lay a piece of fingerpaint paper over the design and then let her gently rub back and forth over the top of the paper to pick up the design. Slowly lift up the paper, turn it over, and look at the print.

# Painted String Sculpture

## Materials

Twine
White glue/liquid starch
Waxed paper
Small containers
Tempera paint

## Preparation

✓ Pour different colors of tempera paint into the small containers.

✓ Mix a little glue with each color.

## Activity

Set the twine, bowls of paint, and waxed paper on the art table. When a child comes to art help him cut a piece of twine and waxed paper. Have him dip his twine into one of the paints, pull it out, and then lay it on the piece of waxed paper. Let him twist and turn the string around until it forms a design he likes. Let the string sculpture dry and then hang from your ceiling.

**HINT:** *If there is too much paint on the string, have the child slide his thumb and forefinger down the string to remove the excess.*

**VARIATION:** *After each child has formed his string design let him make a print of it by laying a piece of white paper over it and rubbing it with his hand. Carefully lift it up. Look at the string design and the print.*

# Palm Printing

## Materials

Dirt
Water in a small pitcher
Large bowl
Heavy-duty spoon
Large meat trays
Mural paper

## Preparation

✓ Do this activity inside or outside.

✓ Dig up a clump of dirt. Put it in a large bowl. Have a child pour water very slowly into the dirt. Let other children stir until the dirt is a thick mud consistency. Scoop the mud onto several large meat trays. Let the children flattened it out.

✓ Cut the mural paper into a large square.

## Activity

Either inside or outside lay the mural paper on a table. Set the mud around the edges. Have the children press their palms into the mud and then make palm prints on the paper. "Is it hard to keep your fingers clean?" Write the children's names near their prints.

# Partner Painting

## Materials

Tempera paint

Small containers such as tuna cans

Small spoons

Newspaper

## Preparation

✓ Pour different colors of tempera paint into the small containers.

✓ Add a little water to each color so that each is fairly thin.

✓ Put a spoon in each container.

✓ Open the newspaper and separate the sheets.

## Activity

Put the paint and newspaper on the art table. Have the children work as partners or a child and adult pair up. Let them take a piece of newspaper off of the stack and set it on the art table. Spoon colors of paint on the newspaper, lift it up and together begin tipping it slowly in all directions, letting the different colors "run" all over the paper and mix together. Let the children spoon more paint if they would like and continue Partner Painting.

# Paste Fingerpainting

## Materials

White paste
Dry tempera/food coloring
Water
Small containers with lids
Small spoons
Cookie sheets

## Preparation

✓ Put paste into small containers.

✓ Add dry tempera/food coloring to each container of paste and stir it in. Add more for a stronger color. (You may prefer to have the children help you mix the colors.)

✓ Cover the containers so that the paste does not dry out.

✓ Pour a little water into several small containters.

## Activity

Set the cookie sheets, water, and paste on the art table. Let the children spoon colored paste on the cookie sheets and fingerpaint. If you are using very large cookie sheets, encourage the children to fingerpaint together. What happens when they mix the colors? Bump their fingers?

**HINT:** *If the paste is getting a little dry, have the children dip their fingers in the water and 'flick' water on the paste and continue to fingerpaint.*

# Pendulum Painting

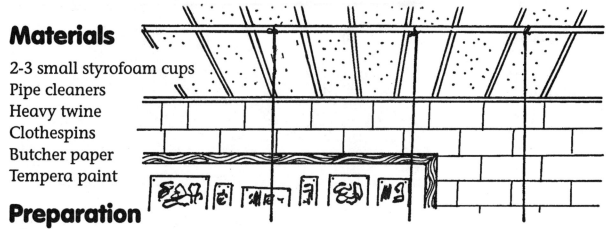

## Materials

2-3 small styrofoam cups
Pipe cleaners
Heavy twine
Clothespins
Butcher paper
Tempera paint

## Preparation

✓ Punch 2 holes opposite each other in each of the cups. Attach a pipe cleaner handle between the holes.

✓ Punch a small hole in the bottom of each cup.

✓ Measure and cut 2-3 pieces of twine to hang down from your ceiling to about 6 inches above your art table. Tie a clothespin to each piece of twine. Hang the twine about 2-3 feet apart over your art table.

✓ Clip a cup to each clothespin.

✓ Pour different colors of paint into small pitchers.

✓ Cut a piece of butcher paper the length of your art table.

## Activity

Lay the piece of butcher paper on the art table. When a child wants to paint she can pour a little paint into one of the cups, wait a second for the paint to begin dripping and then wiggle and shake the cup around to make a design. Fill again and paint some more. As the children paint, the mural will become full of color, zigs, zags and blobs.

**HINT:** *You may have to add water to your tempera paint or enlarge the holes so that paint 'drips' from the cups more easily.*

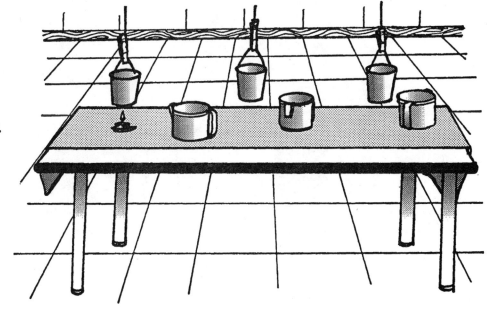

# Popsicle Painting

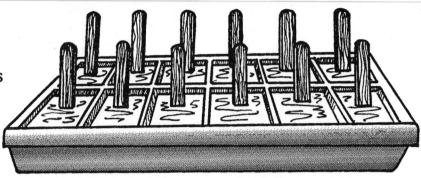

## Materials

Popsicle sticks
Small spoons or scoops
Dry tempera paint
Small containers like margarine tubs
White paper

## Preparation

✓ Make several trays of ice cubes. When the cubes have partially hardened, put a popsicle stick or plastic fork in each one for a handle.

✓ Pour different colors of dry tempera paint into small containers. Put a spoon into each container.

## Activity

Just before you offer the activity, pop the ice cubes out of the trays. Put them in a bucket. Put the bucket and containers of dry paint on the art table. Have the paper nearby.

Have the children take paper and lay it on the art table. Then let them scoop little amounts of tempera paint onto spoons and sprinkle it all over their paper. Repeat until they have the colors they want. Then take one or two ice cubes and smear the ice through the dry paint making colorful designs. Let the paintings dry and then shake off the excess dry tempera paint.

# Powdered Paint Printing

## Materials

Large shallow container
like a brownie pan
Several small pitchers
Dry tempera paint
Salt shakers
Newspaper
White paper

## Preparation

✓ Fill the pitchers about half full of water.

✓ Fill the salt shakers with different colors of dry tempera paint.

✓ If necessary, cut the white paper so that it easily fits in the large container.

## Activity

Set the pitchers of water, large container, and salt shakers on the art table. Have the white paper nearby. Have the children help you lay newspaper on the floor near the art table.

Have a child pour water into the large container so that it is about half to three-quarters full. Let another child sprinkle dry tempera on top of the water. (Some will sink.) After he's sprinkled the colors he wants, let him gently lay a piece of paper on the design and leave it there for a few seconds. If the paper begins to curl, simply poke it down. Lift the paper out of the water. Turn it right-side-up, look at the print, and then lay it on the newspaper to dry.

When each child wants to print, let him sprinkle more tempera on the water and print his design. If the water gets too 'mucky', dump it out, wash the container, pour fresh water into it, and continue.

**VARIATION:** *Instead of using dry tempera paint, use food coloring. Fill the container with water as described; then using a medicine dropper, dot the water with color. Make prints.*

# Prop Painting

## Materials

Printing implements:

> Berry baskets
> Bottle caps
> Corn cobs
> Corrugated pieces
> Film canisters
> Funnels
> Styrofoam chunks
> Spools
> Wooden chunks

Large meat trays
Tempera paint
Paper towels
Large tray
Construction paper

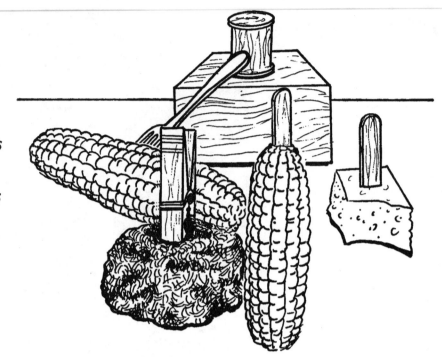

## Preparation

✓ Attach a handle of some type to each object which the children have difficulty holding.

✓ Put all of the printing props on the large tray.

✓ Make different colored printing pads. To make each pad:

**1.** Fold several paper towels together so that they form a thick pad which fits on a meat tray.

**2.** Set the paper towel pad on the meat tray. Slowly pour paint over the pad.

**3.** Roll the paint into the towel with a roller. You want your pad to be moist, but not too soggy.

**4.** Repeat the process for each printing pad.

## Activity

Put the tray of printing props and the printing pads on the art table. Have the construction paper nearby. Encourage the children to print with as many objects and colors as they would like.

*HINT:* Add more paint to the printing pads as necessary,

*VARIATION:* Collect different 'printing props' as you go about your daily experiences. Each time you set-up the activity vary the props.

*VARIATION:* Cut butcher paper the length of your art table and let the children paint a prop mural.

# Pull Painting

## Materials

Large, shallow container
like a brownie pan
Several small pitchers
Dry tempera paint
Salt shakers
Newspapers
Spoons
Clothesline
Clothespins
White paper

## Preparation

✓ Fill the pitchers about
half full of water.

✓ Fill the salt shakers with
different colors of dry tempera paint.

✓ If necessary cut the white paper so
that it easily fits in the large container.

✓ String the clothesline near the art
table and lay newspapers on the floor under it.

## Activity

Set the pitchers of water, large container, and salt shakers on the table. Have
the white paper nearby.

Have a child pour water into the large container so that it is about half to
three-quarters full and then sprinkle it with dry tempera paint.  (Some will
sink, some will float.) Clip a clothespin to a piece of white paper.

After the tempera has settled a little, dip the paper into the water along one
side of the container and using the clothespin for a handle, drag it slowly
through the water. Bring the paper out of the water, look at both sides, and
hang it up on the clothesline. As other children want to Pull Paint they can
sprinkle more dry tempera on the water and then paint. If the water gets too
'mucky' simply pour it out and add clean water.

**VARIATION:** *Add a little liquid vegetable oil to the water and you'll get a slightly
marbleized look.*

# Pump Painting

## Materials

Small bellows
Simple bicycle pump
Small containers
Small spoons
Tempera paint
Butcher paper

## Preparation

✓ Water-down the different colors of tempera paint until they are very watery. Pour the paint into small containers.

✓ Put a spoon in each container.

✓ Cut the butcher paper the length of your art table.

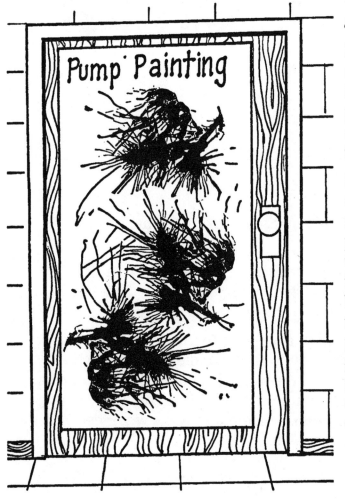

## Activity

Lay the butcher paper on the art table/floor. Write "Pump Painting" at the top. Set the paint containers, bellows and/or bicycle pumps around the paper.

Let the children spoon puddles of paint on the paper. (If necessary show them how to pump the bellows.) Encourage them to blow the paint around the paper by pumping the bellows at different speeds. If the children are blowing the paint around with bicycle pumps, have them work in pairs. One child holds the hose and the other one pumps. After awhile they can switch.

# Pumpkin Rind Printing

## Materials

Pumpkin
Orange tempera paint
Wide brown mailing paper
Forks (optional)

## Preparation

✓ Cut the top off of your pumpkin. Clean and save it. Help the children clean out the rest of the pumpkin. Put the 'meat and seeds' in a separate bowl. Remembering safety, cut the pumpkin in half and then into lots of different size and shape pieces. Put the pieces in a bowl.

✓ Poke a fork into each piece so that each is easier to hold.

✓ Pour orange paint onto trays or into pie pans. Set several pumpkin shapes on each tray.

## Activity

Roll the mailing paper out on the table/floor. Set the paint trays around the paper. Let the children use the pumpkin shapes to make lots of prints. Remember to add more paint to the trays as necessary.

**VARIATION:** *Instead of using orange paint, use red and yellow paint on each tray and let the children mix the paint, if they want.*

# Rain Painting

## Materials

Old white bedsheet
Tempera paint cakes
Newspaper

## Preparation

✓ Put the tempera paint cakes on small meat trays.

## Activity

On a rainy day lay a bedsheet outside in an open area. When it is thoroughly wet, bring it inside and spread it over your art table. Lay newspaper around the floor to catch the drips from the sheet. Put the tempera paint cakes on the sheet.

Let the children paint the sheet by using the tempera paint cakes to make rubbings, designs, fingerprints, and smears.

**HINT:** *If the sheet begins to dry too soon simply spray it with water and continue.*

**EXTENSION:** *After the sheet has been painted and is completely dry, drape it over several chairs or a table for a special tent.*

# Record Player Painting

## Materials

Old record player

White paper/thin 9" or 12" paper plates

Unbreakable eyedroppers

Tempera paints

Small containers like tuna cans

## Preparation

✓ Water down the different colors of tempera paint and pour them into small containers.

✓ Put several eyedroppers into each container.

✓ Cut the white paper into 9" or 12" circles.

✓ Using a pencil, poke a hole in the middle of each circle or paper plate.

## Activity

Put the record player, paint, and paper on the art table. (Tape the record player cord to the floor for safety.) Have a child put a piece of paper on the record player just as if it were a record. Turn the record player on. As the paper is spinning around let her use the eyedroppers to drop colors of paint on the paper. Continue for as long as she'd like.

When finished stop the record player and look at the painting. If she'd like to add more paint, simply start the record player again and continue painting. If not, carefully take the paper off of the record player and set it aside to dry.

**HINT:** *If you set up this activity so that children do it one at a time have a clipboard with paper and pencil. Have children 'sign- up' if they want to do the activity. As each child is finished, have her cross her name off of the list, and ask the next child if he is ready to paint. Remember, they can sign-up as many times as they'd like or change their minds when it is their turn.*

# Roll Along Painting

## Materials

Variety of rolling utensils:
- *Miniature cars*
- *Furniture castors*
- *Brayers*
- *Roller Bottles*

Tempera paint

Meat trays

Variety of paper:
- *Butcher paper*
- *Brown mailing paper*
- *Shelf paper*
- *Construction paper*

## Preparation

✓ Pour different colors of tempera paint into the meat trays.

✓ Cut the butcher paper the length of your art table.

✓ Fill roller bottles with different colors of paint.

## Activity

Offer one type of roller utensil each time you do this activity. Lay the paper on the art table/floor. Set the trays of paint and the rolling utensils around the edges of the paper. Have children roll the utensils in the paint and then roll color on the paper.

***VARIATION:*** *On Different Days Offer:*

- ■ *Miniature cars on butcher paper or large maps*
- ■ *Castors on brown mailing paper*

- ■ *Brayers on shelf paper*
- ■ *Roller bottles on construction paper*

# Rolling Pin Painting

## Materials

Different sizes of rolling pins
Textured rolling pins (optional)
Spoons
Small containers
Large meat trays
Tempera paint
Newspaper

## Preparation

✓ Pour different colors of tempera paint into the small containers.

✓ Put a spoon in each container.

✓ Unfold the sheets of newspaper, cut them if they are too large, and then stack them.

## Activity

Put the rolling pins on the meat trays and set them on the art table along with the containers of paint. Set the newspaper nearby.

When children want to paint have them take pieces of newspaper, lay them on the art table/floor, and spoon different colors of paint on them. After they have put color on their newspapers, let them use different rolling pins to roll the paint all over the paper. Maybe they would like to add more paint and then roll some more.

**VARIATION:** *Instead of spooning the paint onto the newspaper, spoon it onto the rolling pins, and then roll the 'painted pins' on the newspapers.*

# Rubber Ball Painting

## Materials

3-4 rubber balls the size of baseballs
3-4 large margarine tubs
3-4 spoons
Tempera paint
Bedsheet

## Preparation

✓ Pour different colors of tempera paint into the margarine tubs.
✓ Put a spoon and rubber ball in each tub.

## Activity

Drape the bedsheet over your art table or lay it on the floor. Put the tubs of paint on the sheet. Have the children work in pairs. One child should roll a ball around in the paint, set it on the bedsheet, and then gently roll it to his partner. The partner stops it, adds more paint, and rolls it back again. The children continue dipping and rolling the rubber balls around the sheet.

**HINT:** *The floor is easier for younger children.*

78

# Rubber Band Printing

## Materials

All widths of
rubber bands
Pieces of wood
Tempera paint
Construction paper

## Preparation

✓ Pour a little
   tempera paint
   into meat trays or
   pie pans.

✓ Put a variety of
   rubber bands on
   several trays.

✓ Sand the rough
   edges off of your
   pieces of wood and
   put them in a wash
   tub.

## Activity

Set the construction paper, wood, trays of rubber bands, and paint on the art table.
Show the children how to wrap rubber bands around the wood and then let them
wrap as many as they would like and in whichever direction.

Have the children dip their blocks in the paint and print designs on their paper.
Encourage them to print as many designs and colors as they would like.

79

# Rubber Finger Fingerpainting

## Materials

Small containers
Small spoons
Rubber fingers (small size which you can purchase in any office supply store)
Fingerpaint
Plastic trays

## Preparation

✓ Spoon different colors of fingerpaint into small containers.

✓ Put a small spoon in each container.

✓ Put the rubber fingers in a pie pan or meat tray.

## Activity

Set the containers of fingerpaint, rubber fingers, and plastic trays on the art table. Have the children take trays and rubber fingers when they come to art. Let them put the 'fingers' on any of their fingers. Wiggle their fingers around. How do the rubber fingers feel? Add more fingers if they'd like or change the ones they have to other fingers.

Let them spoon paint onto their trays and then fingerpaint. Look at their designs. Can they tell which strokes they made with rubber fingers and real fingers? Maybe they would like to switch the rubber fingers around or add several more. Continue fingerpainting.

# Salt Shaker Painting

## Materials

Liquid tempera paint

Clean unbreakable
salt/pepper shakers

Newspaper

## Preparation

✓ Carefully pour each color of paint into a salt/pepper shaker.

✓ Unfold the newspaper so that it is flat.

## Activity

Put the salt/pepper shakers filled with paint on the art table/floor. Have the children lay their sheets of newspaper down. Hold the salt/pepper shakers upside down and shake them with firm jerking motions. Watch the paint 'hit' the paper. Shake again and again. Let children paint for as long as they want. Maybe some children will want to hold a shaker in each hand and shake both of them together.

*VARIATION: Pour paint into small pitchers. Poke holes in the bottom of small paper cups. Let children pour paint into the cups and shake them over newspaper.*

# Sandy Painting

## Materials

Sand
Small containers such as tuna cans
Tempera paint
Wooden spoons
Small spoons
Forks (optional)
Cardboard

## Preparation

✓ Put different colors of tempera paint into small containers. Let the children mix a little sand into each color.

✓ Cut your cardboard into individual pieces.

## Activity

Put the sandy paint, small spoons, and wooden spoons on the art table. Set the cardboard pieces nearby. Let children lay cardboard in front of them, scoop paint onto small spoons, and drizzle it over the paper. Repeat with different colors and/or more of the same color.

After the paint has been drizzled, let the children use wooden spoons to blend the colors, crunch the sand, and spread the paint. (Use the forks to add more design.)

After the paint has dried encourage the children to look at and gently feel their Sandy Paintings. What do they think?

**EXTENSION:** *You might have pieces of sandpaper available for the children to feel and compare to their paintings.*

**VARIATION:** *Instead of sand use salt or dried coffee grounds.*

# Slippery Mud Fingerpainting

## Materials

Dirt
Water
Liquid starch
Large mixing bowl
Mixing spoon
Liquid dish detergent
Large unbreakable trays
Paper towels
Spray bottle of water

## Preparation

✓ Make the Slippery Mud. You may want to do this with your children.

**1.** Mix dirt and a little water to make a thick mud.

**2.** Add a little liquid starch and dish detergent. Stir the ingredients until they are thoroughly mixed.

**3.** Cover the mixture until the children are ready to use it.

## Activity

Put the bowl of Slippery Mud, trays, paper towels, and spray bottle of water on the art table. Have the children take trays, scoop a little Slippery Mud onto them, and begin to fingerpaint. When the children finish fingerpainting, have them spray a little water on their hands and wipe them dry with paper towels.

*EXTENSION:* *As children are fingerpainting talk about how the mud feels and smells. Do they see anything else in the mud such as sticks, stones, leaves, grasses?*

# Smear And Draw Painting

## Materials

Packing foam
Clothespins
Drawing utensils:
*Round toothpicks*
*Popsicle sticks*
*Coffee stirrers*
*Cotton swabs*
*Unsharpened pencils*
Tempera paint
Construction paper
Medium size containers

## Preparation

✓ Make Foam Daubers:
1. Cut the piece of foam into 2" squares.
2. Clip a clothespin onto each one.

✓ Pour tempera paint into small containers.

✓ Put several foam daubers in each paint container.

✓ Put all of the drawing utensils on a large tray.

## Activity

Put the paint containers with daubers and drawing utensils on the art table. Have the construction paper nearby.

As children want to paint have them take a piece of paper and use the foam daubers to smear as many colors of paint over their paper as they would like. While the paint is wet, encourage the children to use the different utensils and make pictures in their paint. If they would like to 'erase' any of their drawings, all they need to do is smear paint over the unwanted lines and continue to draw.

# Smelly Fingerpainting

## Materials

Flour
Water
Small pitchers
Ground cinnamon
Mixing spoon
Large bowl
Small spoons
Plastic trays

## Preparation

✓ Pour the water into small pitchers which the children can easily handle.

## Activity

Bring all of the ingredients to the art table and let the children help you mix the fingerpaint. Scoop flour into the bowl. Let the children slowly pour water into the bowl. As they are pouring, mix the flour and water together. Stop adding water to the mixture when it becomes the right consistency for fingerpaint. Add more flour and water if you want more fingerpaint. Now let each child shake a little cinnamon into the fingerpaint. SMELL! AAAAAHH! Slowly stir the cinnamon into the mixture.

As the children want to fingerpaint, have them spoon some of the mixture onto a tray and then paint. Add more paint if they want and fingerpaint some more.

**VARIATION:** *Make fingerpaint using this recipe, but substitute a different 'smell' for the cinnamon each time you mix it. (peppermint, vanilla, dried coffee grounds, etc.)*

# Snow Painting

## Materials

Dry tempera paint

Unbreakable salt/pepper shakers

White construction paper

## Preparation

✓ Put different colors of dry tempera paint into salt/pepper shakers.

## Activity

Do this activity on a snowy day.

Put the shakers of dry tempera paint on the art table. Have construction paper nearby. Let the children shake as many different colors of dry paint as they would like on their paper. Carefully put the papers in a secluded place.

When the children are dressed to go outside for awhile, let those who've begun their paintings go get them and carry them outside. Let the children set their paintings in a place where the snow will fall on them, but yet no one is actively playing. As everyone is playing watch what happens to the paintings. Carry them back inside if enough snow has fallen on them; if not, leave them outside for awhile longer.

# Soapy Fingerpainting

## Materials

Clothes soap powder
Water
Large spoon
Tempera paint
Liquid soap pump bottles
Large unbreakable trays
Large mixing bowl with lid
Paper towels

## Preparation

✓ Pour several different colors of paint into different pump bottles.

✓ Mix a big batch of Soapy Fingerpaint. You may want to mix it with your children.

    1. Pour 4 cups of powdered soap into a large bowl.
    2. Pour 2 cups of water into the bowl.
    3. Slowly stir the ingredients together.
    4. Cover the bowl until the children are ready to use it.

## Activity

Put the trays, large spoon, batch of soapy fingerpaint, and paint pumps on the art table.

When a child wants to fingerpaint, have her take a tray, scoop some Soapy Fingerpaint on it, and begin to fingerpaint. After awhile encourage her to add color to her fingerpaint by pumping a little paint onto the tray and then continuing to fingerpaint. Add another color and scoop a little more fingerpaint. Continue until the child is finished; then have her clean her tray by wiping it with paper towels. Now it is ready for another child.

# Sponge Painting

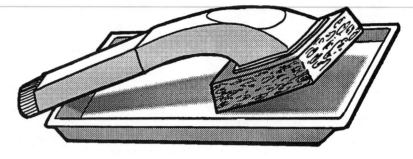

## Materials

Dish sponges with handles
Tempera paint
Butcher paper

## Preparation

✓ Water-down several colors of tempera paint. Pour one color into each sponge handle.

✓ Cut the butcher paper the length of your art table.

## Activity

Lay the paper on your art table/floor. Put each sponge on a small meat tray and set the trays on the paper. Let the children use the sponges to make prints and designs all over the paper.

**VARIATION:** *Cut giant sponges into different shapes. Have small tubs of colored water. Take the supplies outside and let the children make prints on your sidewalk.*

# Sponge Squeeze Painting

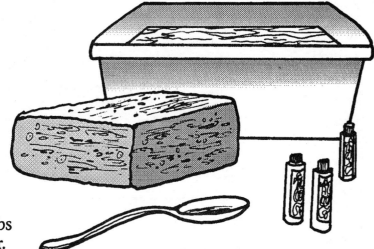

## Materials

Buckets or dish tubs
Food coloring
Giant sponges
Big spoons

## Preparation

✓ Fill several buckets/tubs about 3/4 full of water.

## Activity

Carry the tubs of water outside and set them on a sidewalk. Have the children carry the food coloring and sponges and put them by the water.

Let a child squeeze a little food coloring into one bucket. Watch the color spread out over the water and then stir it in. Add more coloring until it is the color the children want. Repeat for the other colors.

Put a sponge/s in each tub. When children want to take a break from their active play, encourage them to come over and squeeze colored water designs on the sidewalk.

**VARIATION:** *In addition to the colored water and sponges bring an old white bedsheet. Instead of squeezing designs on the sidewalk, have the children do it on the sheet. Let the sheet dry and then use it for a class wall hanging or for a canopy or tent in your play area.*

# Spool Painting

## Materials

Variety of spools:
   *Thread*
   *Ribbon*
   *Wire*
Hangers with
cardboard tubes
Meat trays
Tempera paint
Newspaper

## Preparation

✓  Make your Spool Rollers:

**1.** Take the cardboard tubes off of each hanger. (HINT: Save the tubes for other activities. You could tie brightly colored scarves on them and use for scarf dancing.)

**2.** Cut the excess wire from each side so that they are about 5-6 inches long.

**3.** Bend the tips of each wire to form a right angle.

**4.** Put a spool between the ends of the wires and clamp it in.

**5.** Roll it a little to get the spool rolling around. Tighten or loosen the spool as needed.

**6.** Wrap tape around the handle for safety.

✓  Pour shallow amounts of paint into the meat trays.

✓  Separate the sheets of newspaper, cut them if they are too large, and then stack them.

## Activity

Put the trays of paint and spool rollers on the art table/floor. Set the stack of newspapers nearby.

Have the children take pieces of newspaper and lay them on the table/floor. Take a spool roller, roll it back and forth in the paint, and then roll the paint on the newspaper. Continue, filling the roller with paint and rolling it on the newspaper. Encourage the children to change colors of paint and rollers.

# Spoon And Roll Painting

## Materials

Rolling pins
Small containers
Small spoons/scoops
Tempera paint
Light colored construction paper

## Preparation

✓ Pour different colors of tempera paint into the small containers.

✓ Put at least one spoon/scoop in each container.

Raz

Raz made a print.

## Activity

Set the containers of paint and rolling pins on the art table. Put the construction paper nearby. Let each child take a piece of paper and spoon all colors of paint onto it. Lay a second sheet of construction paper over the first one, and then use a rolling pin to roll over the top sheet. After rolling, separate the two sheets.

*VARIATION: Lay a sheet of butcher paper on the art table. Have the children spoon paint on a section of the large piece, lay a piece of construction paper over their paint drops, and then roll over it with a rolling pin. Carefully lift up the piece of construction paper. Look at the section of butcher paper and the matching construction paper.*

91

# Spray Bottle Painting

## Materials

Food coloring
Spray bottles
Clothespins
Butcher paper

## Preparation

✓ Mix colored water with the children. (If you prefer use watered-down tempera paint.) Pour each color into a spray bottle.

✓ Cut a long sheet of butcher paper and roll it up to carry outside.

## Activity

Have the children help you carry the art materials outside. Hang the butcher paper low on the fence. Set the spray bottles of colored water along the fence.

When the children feel like taking a break from their active play, encourage them to paint the mural by spraying color on it.

**EXTENSION:** *As the mural develops watch the colors change, the colored water drip, and the mural in various states of wet and dry.*

# Squeeze Bottle Painting

## Materials

Squeeze bottles (like ketchup/mustard)
Tempera paint
Flour
Wallpaper

## Preparation

✓ Thicken your tempera paint. (You may prefer to do this with the children.)
   1. Pour one color of paint into a large bowl.
   2. Slowly stir flour into the paint, thickening it until it is fairly thick.
✓ Pour the thickened paint into squeeze bottles.

## Activity

Put the squeeze bottles, wallpaper, and scissors on the art table. As the children come to the art table to paint, let them (or you) cut pieces of wallpaper off of the roll and lay them on the table. Let the children use as many different colors of paint as they would like as they create their paintings. You may need to tape the paper down to prevent it from curling up.

**HINT:** *Refill the squeeze bottles as necessary. When they get less than 1/4 full, they become difficult to squeeze because the paint is so thick.*

# Squeeze Painting

## Materials

Ketchup, detergent, or other squeeze bottles
Small containers
Small spoons
Tempera paint
Butcher paper

## Preparation

✓ Water-down the different colors of tempera paint until they are very watery.

✓ Pour the paint into small containers.

✓ Put a small spoon in each container.

✓ Cut the butcher paper the length of your art table.

## Activity

Lay the butcher paper on the art table/floor. Write "Squeeze Bottle Painting" at the top. Set the paint containers and squeeze bottles around the paper. Have the children spoon small puddles of the same or different colors of paint on the paper. Holding the squeeze bottles near the paint have them squeeze the bottles and blow the paint all around the paper. What happens when two colors mix?

Let the paint dry, and then hang the mural at the children's eye level. Have fun looking at all of the colors.

# Squiggle Painting

## Materials

Heavy-weight string/twine
Spring-loaded clothespins
Meat trays
Tempera paint
Construction paper

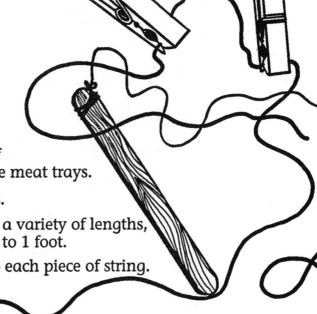

## Preparation

✓ Pour different colors of
   tempera paint onto the meat trays.

✓ Make Clothespin Clips.

   1. Cut the strings into a variety of lengths,
      ranging from 6 inches to 1 foot.

   2. Clip a clothespin to each piece of string.

## Activity

Put the trays of tempera paint on the art table. Place several 'Clothespin
Clips' in each color. Have the construction paper nearby.

When children come to art have them put paper on the art table, squiggle
clothespin clips in the tempera, and then paint their papers with the paint-
filled strings. Encourage them to squiggle, bounce, flick, and pull the strings
to get different designs on their papers.

**VARIATION:** *If you have young children, tie the string to popsicle sticks rather
than spring-loaded clothespins.*

# Statue Painting

## Materials

Large plastic trash bags
Newspaper
Sponges
Clothespins
Meat trays
Liquid dish detergent
Tempera paint

## Preparation

✓ Make Sponge Daubers
   1. Cut a large sponge into small pieces.
   2. Clip a clothespin to each one.

✓ Pour tempera paint into small containers and mix several squirts of liquid detergent into each one. (This will make the tempera paint adhere to the slippery surface of the trash bags.)

✓ Pour shallow amounts of the different colors of paint onto meat trays.

✓ Stack the sheets of newspaper.

## Activity

This activity is a two step process.

**Step 1:** Construct the Statues.

Have children work together. They should wad up the sheets of newspaper and stuff plastic bags. Stuff the bags full so they are tight and plump, and let the air out before closing them up with a twistem or rubber band.

**Step 2:** Paint the Statues.

Lay newspaper on the floor or art table. Set the statues on the newspaper. Put the paint trays and sponge daubers near each statue. Let the children paint each statue as they want.

**HINT:** *Refill the paint trays as necessary. Because of the slippery surface the paint easily runs. By keeping the paint shallow, the sponge daubers do not get overly saturated with paint.*

# Stop And Go Fingerpainting

## Materials

Record player
Favorite music
Small containers
Small spoons
Fingerpaint
Fingerpaint paper

## Preparation

✓ Put different colors of fingerpaint into small containers.

✓ Put a small spoon in each container.

## Activity

Put the fingerpaint paper, the record player, and record near the art table. Set the fingerpaint containers on the table. When the children want to paint, have them put their papers on the table and spoon the fingerpaint on them. Start the music!

Let the children paint to the beat of the music. Stop the music. The children who are painting should 'freeze.' They can add more fingerpaint to their paintings if they want. Start the music again and continue painting. Continue painting and freezing. Maybe you'll want to change the music and let the children paint to a different beat.

# Straw Painting

## Materials

Wide-mouth straws
Small containers
Small spoons
Tempera paint
Waste basket
Butcher paper

## Preparation

✓ Water-down the different colors of tempera paint until they are very watery. Pour the paint into small containers.

✓ Put a small spoon in each container.

✓ Cut the straws in half and put them on a meat tray.

✓ Set the waste basket near the table.

✓ Cut the butcher paper the length of your art table.

## Activity

Lay the butcher paper on the art table/floor. Set the paint containers around the paper. Put the straws off to the side. Let each child get a straw, spoon a small puddle of paint on the paper, and then blow it around. Keep blowing. Add more paint and blow again. When each child is finished have her throw her straw in the waste basket. You may want to leave the activity set-up for several days. If you do, change the colors of paint. If you have older children you could also let them use a regular width straw. Take this opportunity to talk about the differences.

# String Dip Painting

## Materials

Heavy string/twine
Tempera paint
White glue
Small containers like tuna cans
Construction paper
White paper

## Preparation

✓ Cut short pieces of string and lay them on several meat trays. (If your children can cut string let them cut their own pieces.)

✓ Pour different colors of tempera paint into the small containers.

✓ Mix a little white glue with each one.

## Activity

Put the string, scissors if necessary, and containers of paint on the art table. Set the construction paper and white paper nearby.

As a child wants to paint, let her lay a piece of contruction paper on the art table, dip a piece of string into one of the paints, pull it out and arrange it on her paper. Repeat again and again using different colors and lengths of string.

After each child has finished her String Dip design, ask her if she would like to make a print of it. If so, get a piece of white paper, carefully lay it over the design, and slowly rub over the top of the entire paper. Carefully lift up the top piece of paper. Look at the string design and the print.

# Sun Catcher Painting

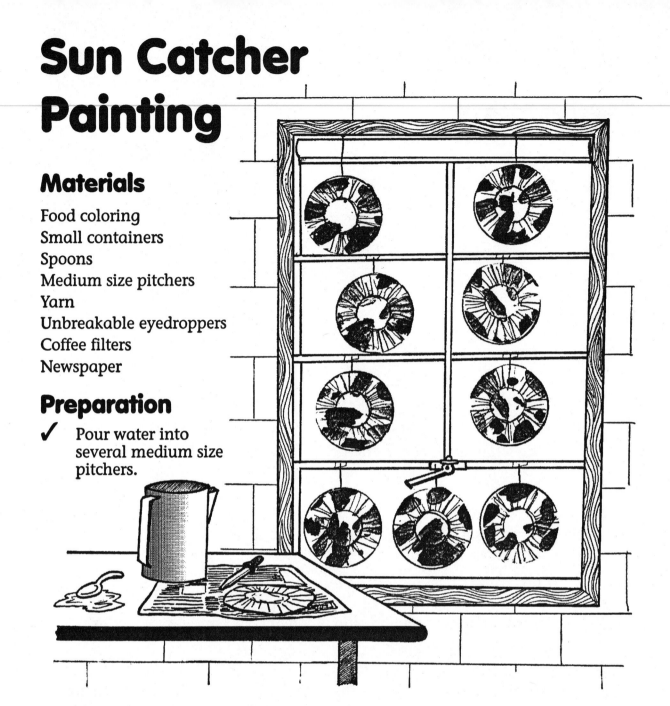

## Materials

Food coloring
Small containers
Spoons
Medium size pitchers
Yarn
Unbreakable eyedroppers
Coffee filters
Newspaper

## Preparation

✓ Pour water into
several medium size
pitchers.

## Activity

Spread newspaper on the art table. Put the water, spoons, small containers, and food coloring on the table. Let the children pour water into each of the containers. Drop several dots of color into the first container. Watch it spread through the water and then have a child stir it. Repeat this activity to make the rest of the colors.

Put small eyedroppers in each color. Let the children paint coffee filters by dripping dots of color on them. As they are painting, it is fun to hold the filters up to the sun or light and see how the colors are affected.

When each child is finished, have her punch a hole near the edge of the filter. Tie a piece of yarn through the hole and then hang it in the window.

# T-Shirt Painting

## Materials

T-shirts
Fabric paint
Meat trays
Small containers with covers
Thick sponges
Popsicle sticks/clothespins
Large sheets of used cardboard
Clothesline
Clothespins
Masking tape
Markers
Hangers

## Preparation

✓ Pour each color of fabric paint into a small container. Mix a little water with each one. Cover each container until you're ready to paint.

✓ Cut the sponges into various sizes.

✓ Cut a small slit into each sponge shape and insert a popsicle stick handle into each one. (You could add a dot of glue or use your hot glue gun to adhere the stick to the sponge better. Safety.)

✓ String the clothesline in a quiet place. (If outside, hang the T-shirts on your fence.)

## Activity

Do this activity inside or outside.

Pour shallow amounts of fabric paint into the meat trays and set them on the art table/floor. Have a child slip a piece of cardboard between the front and back of her shirt and then, using the different sponges and colors, paint a design on the front.

When she is finished, write her name on a piece of masking tape and stick it to her shirt. Carefully pull the cardboard out, put the shirt on a hanger, and hook it on the clothesline or fence to dry.

**VARIATION:** *Great activity for your all-school picnic, family gathering, or field day.*

# Tape Design Painting

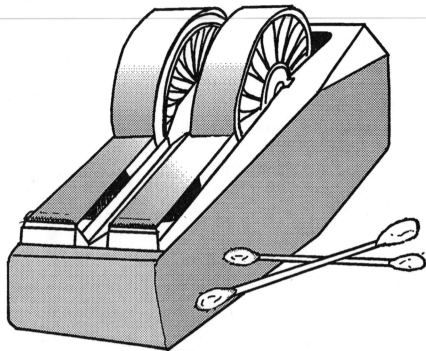

## Materials

Removable adhesive
tape/masking tape
Watercolors
Cotton swabs
White paper

## Preparation

✓ Pour a little water into
small containers.

✓ Put cotton swabs on a
meat tray.

## Activity

Put the water, watercolors, tape, and cotton swabs on the art table. Have the paper nearby.

Have the children lay their paper on the art table and put strips of tape all over it. After they have put as much tape down as they want, encourage them to paint the paper with watercolors. Set the art off to the side to dry.

After the paint has totally dried, let each child carefully pull up the tape and throw it away. Some children may want to add marker or crayon drawings to their designs.

# Textured Can Printing

## Materials

Heavy string
Liquid white glue
Juice cans
Large meat trays
Tempera paint
Paper grocery bags

## Preparation

✓ **Day 1** - Pour glue into small margarine tubs.

✓ **Day 2** - Pour shallow amounts of different colors of paint onto the meat trays.

## Activity

This is a two-day activity. (If your children are young or you prefer, make the textured cans ahead of time.)

**Day 1** - Set the juice cans and glue on the art table. Have the string nearby. Let each child decide how long he wants his string. Cut it. Have him dip his string into the glue, pull it out, and then squeeze the excess glue off by holding the string at the top with one hand and sliding his thumb and forefinger from his other hand down the string. The excess glue will drip back into the margarine tub. Now have the child wrap the sticky string around and around his can. Let the cans dry overnight.

**Day 2** - Set the grocery bags, paint, and texture cans on the table. Let the children roll the cans in the paint and then print on the paper bags. Re-dip and roll some more. Use as many colors as they would like.

# Textured Fingerpainting

## Materials

Different colors of fingerpaint
Small containers
Spoons
Cookie sheets
Variety of textures:
    *Sand*
    *Dried coffee grounds*
    *Aquarium gravel*
    *Baking powder*
    *Cornmeal*
    *Cornstarch*
    *Liquid soap*
    *Sawdust*
    *Sugar*
    *Whole cloves*

## Preparation

✓ Choose one type of texture and gather enough to add to your fingerpaint.

## Activity

Spoon the fingerpaint into small containers. Have the children add 'texture' to each container and then stir it into the paint.

When children want to fingerpaint, have them spoon the textured paint onto a cookie sheet and fingerpaint. How does it feel? Does it smell?

**VARIATION:** *Use other textures in your fingerpaint. As children paint, talk about the similarities and differences.*

# Thick Paint Painting

## Materials

Flour
Water
Popsicle sticks
Spoons
Large margarine tubs with lids
Dry tempera paint
Uncoated cardboard

## Preparation

✓ Make your thick paint: You may prefer to do this with the children.

1. In a large bowl mix one color of dry tempera paint with a little flour.

2. Slowly add water to the mixture, stirring constantly. Continue adding water until the mixture is the consistency of paste. Put a lid on the container if you are not going to use the paint right away.

3. Repeat the process for each color.

✓ Put a spoon in each tub of paint.

✓ Cut the cardboard into different size and shape pieces.

## Activity

Put the paint, popsicle sticks and cardboard on the art table. Let the children spoon paint onto their cardboard pieces and then use the popsicle sticks to smear it around.

**DISPLAY:** *After the paintings have dried, mount each one on a piece of colored construction paper. Hang them on a bulletin board or wall.*

# Thumbs Up Printing

## Materials

Ink pads
Additional ink
Easel paper
Magnifying glasses
(Optional)

## Preparation

✓ If you do not have ink pads make your own. You'll need paper towels, small meat trays, and tempera paint. To make each pad:

1. Fold a paper towel so that it fits on a meat tray.

2. Set the folded towel on the tray. Pour a little paint on the towel.

3. Roll the paint into the towel with a brayer or wallpaper seam roller.

4. Repeat the process for each printing pad.

## Activity

Lay a piece of easel paper on the art table. Put several colors of ink pads around the paper. Encourage the children to make thumb and finger prints all over the paper. Label the children's prints.

**EXTENSION:** *Set the easel paper in the science area with several magnifying glasses. Leave it there for several days so that the children can examine all of their prints. Look again and again to find similarities and differences.*

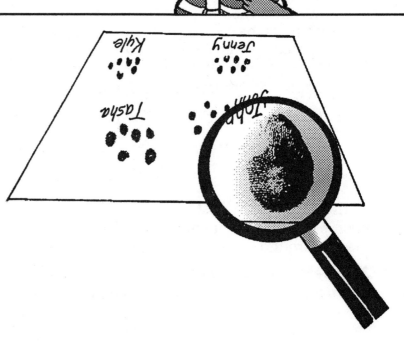

# Toast Painting

## Materials

Bread
Milk
Food coloring
Toaster
Small containers
Cotton swabs
Spoons

## Preparation

✓ Pour the milk into a small pitcher.

✓ Put the cotton swabs on a meat tray.

## Activity

Have children help you mix the colored milk. Let several children pour the milk into the small containers. Add a different color of food coloring to each container. Using different spoons let the children stir the coloring into the milk.

Put the bread, cotton swabs, colored milk, and toaster on the art table. (Tape the toaster cord to the floor for safety.) Let the children paint their pieces of toast with colored milk. As each has finished painting, pop the bread into the toaster. When it pops up, let the child have her special snack along with a glass of juice.

# Tube Painting

## Materials

Variety of sizes of paper tubes
Large meat trays
Tempera paint
Paper plates

## Preparation

✓ Pour shallow amounts
of tempera paint into
the meat trays.

✓ Put the paper tubes
in a large box.

## Activity

Put the paint trays and paper
tubes on the art table. Let the
children roll as many tubes
as they would like in the
different colors. After each
tube is covered with paint
have the child stand it on a
paper plate to dry. After all of
the tubes have thoroughly
dried let the children string
them on several pieces of
long yarn and then hang
them around the room.

**VARIATION:** *Instead of
stringing the colorful tubes use
them to create a giant mobile.
Maybe you could hang it in the
entranceway.*

**VARIATION:** *Stir in a little
glue to each color of paint. Roll
the tubes as described and then
add paper scraps to each one.
Let dry and hang.*

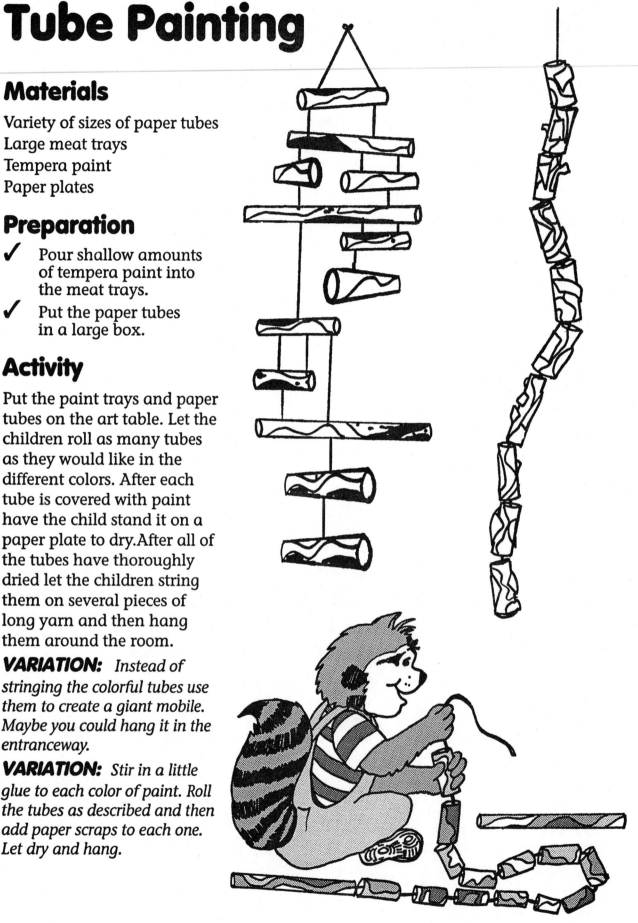

# Wax Resist Painting

## Materials

White crayons, parafin or candles
Cotton swabs
Several small containers
Watercolor paints
White paper

## Preparation

✓ Pour water into the
  containers.

## Activity

Set the white
crayons, cotton
swabs, containers
of water, and
watercolor paints
on the table. Have
the white paper
nearby.

Have a child take a
piece of paper and
draw his design,
scribble or picture
on it with white
crayon. Talk about
where his design is.
Maybe feel the
crayon lines. Have
him watercolor his
paper using cotton
swabs. (Magic -
Can he see his
original drawing?)

# Waxed Paper Painting

## Materials

Waxed paper
White paper
Watercolor markers
Masking tape

## Preparation

✓ | None

## Activity

Put the watercolor markers on the art table. Have the box of waxed paper, white paper, and tape nearby. As each child chooses to paint, have her decide how long a piece of waxed paper she'd like to paint on. Cut the paper. Have her lay it on the table and then tape it down if necessary.

Let her make whatever designs, scribbles, pictures, and so on that she'd like. After she has finished, have her gently lay a piece of paper over her picture, and then softly and slowly rub it with her hand. Lift up the piece of white paper and look at the design. You might want to compare it to the markings and colors on the waxed paper.

**VARIATION:** *Try this activity on different surfaces: extra laminating material, heavy-duty plastic, large freezer bags, fingerpaint paper, and the shiny side of freezer wrap paper.*

# Week-Long Printing

## Materials

Variety of kitchen utensils:
- *Pancake turners*
- *Spatulas*
- *Forks*
- *Apple slicers*
- *Potato mashers*

Tempera paint

Mural paper

*We printed with pancake turners.*

## Preparation

✓ Pour shallow amounts of different colors of tempera paint into pie pans/meat trays.

✓ Cut a sheet of mural paper long enough so that it can be divided into 5 large sections —one section for each type of kitchen utensil.

## Activity

On the first day roll out the mural paper so that one section is available to print on. Set the paint pans around the edges of the paper. Put one type of kitchen utensil in the paint. Let the children print with the different colors and utensils. When finished, label the section.

On the next day roll out the paper so that the children can print with a second type of kitchen utensil in the second section. Continue in this fashion until the mural is finished. After it is dry, hang it up in the hall at the children's eye level.

# Wheeling Around Painting

## Materials

Wide butcher paper
All types of small toy vehicles with different tire treads
Large meat trays
Tempera paint
Paper towels

## Preparation

✓ Cut your butcher paper into a giant track.

✓ Make different colored printing pads. To make each pad:

**1.** Fold several paper towels together so that they form a thick pad which fits on a meat tray.

**2.** Set the paper towel pad on the meat tray. Slowly pour paint over the pad.

**3.** Roll the paint into the towel with a roller. You want your pad to be moist, but not too soggy.

**4.** Repeat the process for each printing pad.

## Activity

Lay the giant track on the floor. Place the printing pads and vehicles around the edge.

Have the children roll their vehicles back and forth on the printing pads and then drive them on the giant track. When the prints get weak, simply roll the vehicles in the paint again and drive some more. When finished hang the giant track on a wall in your hall.

*HINT:* *Add more paint to the printing pads as necessary.*

# Yarn Painting

## Materials

Heavy-weight yarn
Clothespins
Meat trays
Tempera paint
Construction paper

## Preparation

✓ Make Clothespin Clips:

   1. Cut yarn into pieces ranging from six to nine inches long.
   2. Attach a clothespin to each one.

✓ Pour different colors of tempera paint into meat trays.

## Activity

Place the paint trays on the art table. Put at least one clothespin clip in each color. Set the construction paper nearby.

Have each child take a piece of construction paper and fold it in half. Open up the paper. Dip one of the pieces of yarn into the paint, lift it out, and set it on the paper. Fold the paper closed. With one hand hold the paper closed and slowly wiggle the yarn all around until it comes out from between the paper.

After the yarn is out, open the paper and look at the painting. If the child wants to do it again let him use the same color or a different one. Continue until he is finished and then have him set his painting off to the side to dry.

# Painting

**1.** *Respect children's paintings:*

● If you are writing children's names on their paintings, let them tell you where they want their names.

● Display paintings appropriately.

● Let children take their paintings home or display them in the classroom.

● Talk with the children about their paintings.

**2.** *When working with the warming tray:*

● Push it away from the edge of the table so children do not lean on it.

● Tape the cord to the floor.

● Check it often to be sure it is on the lowest temperature.

● Wear mittens or gloves.

**3.** *When fingerpainting...* keep the surface moist so the paint moves easily. Keep a small spray bottle nearby to moisten the surface or children's fingers.

**4.** *When doing a printing activity:*

● Pour shallow layers of paint in containers or on pads.

● Use flat-type containers and trays.

● Add more paint as printing pads become dry.

● Attach handles to objects which are difficult to hold.

**5.** *Help children keep their art organized:*

● Put a large tarp on the floor when doing art on the floor.

● Use small and large washable, unbreakable trays on the art table. (Cookie trays and sheet cake pans.)

● Have washable placemats and heavy-duty wallpaper pieces available.

● Have a wide variety of supplies readily available on the art shelf.

Elgin, Illinois   60123

# Hints

**6.** *Keep clean-up as easy as possible:*

- Let the children clean-up as much as possible.

- Have children wear smocks.

- Add a little liquid dish detergent to your tempera paint.

- Use easy to wash containers.

- Cover your floor if the activity is especially wet or messy.

- Put a spray bottle of water and paper towels near the art table if a sink is not readily available for hand washing.

**7.** *Add handles to art materials which are difficult to control.*

For example:

- Clip clothespins to small sponge pieces. Use chip clips for larger pieces.

- Tie or tape popsicle sticks to string, twine, and yarn.

- Hot glue (or white glue) plastic tops or wooden blocks to cookie cutters, container lids, and puzzle pieces.

- Poke forks into sections of pumpkin rind and pieces of foam.

- Insert popsicle sticks into styrofoam pieces and ice cubes.

**8.** *Remember safety:*

- Keep a mop handy for drying the floor.

- Tape electrical cords to the floor.

- Keep unused electrical plugs covered.

- Set-up activities using electrical appliances in quiet, inactive places in the classroom.

Elgin, Illinois  60123

# Permanent Supplies

Balls
Berry baskets
Castors
Child-size brooms
Child-size mops
Clothesline
Clothespins
Combs
Cookie cutters
Corks
Deodorant bottles
Dish tubs
Eyedroppers
Film canisters
Fly swatters
Forks
Funnels
Gloves
Golf balls
Gym shoes
Hot glue guns
Ice cube trays
Ink pads
Jar lids
Kitchen utensils
Lazy susan plate
Liquid soap pump bottles

Marbles
Mittens
Mixing bowls
Paint rollers
Pie pans
Pitchers
Record player
Rolling pins
Rubber boots
Rubber fingers
Scissors
Sponges
Spoons - small/large
Spray bottles
Squeeze bottles
Toaster
Toy vehicles
Types of surfaces
  *Brownie pans*
  *Bubble pack*
  *Carpet protectors*
  *Cookie sheets*
  *Linoleum*
  *Plastic placemats*
  *Plastic trays*
  *Rubber bath mats*
  *Sheet cake pans*
Tuna cans
Warming tray

Elgin, Illinois 60123

# Disposable Supplies

All types paper
Aluminum foil
Appliance boxes
Bedsheets
Bubbles
Candles
Cardboard
Chalk
Clothes soap powder
Cotton batting/swabs
Craft sticks
Crayons
Cylinder boxes
Dirt
Dish detergent
Dixie cups
Egg cartons
Fabric
Foam insulation tape
Foods
  *Corn Starch*
  *Evaporated milk*
  *Flour*
  *Ground cinnamon*
  *Peppermint extract*
  *Vanilla extract*
Food coloring
Juice cans
Large trash bags

Liquid starch
Masking tape
Metal hangers
Packing foam
Paint
Paper tubes
Paraffin
Paste
Pencils
Pipe cleaners
Popsicle sticks/craft sticks
Removable tape
Ribbon
Rubber bands
Sand
Shallow boxes
Shaving cream
Spools
Styrofoam cups
Styrofoam trays
Tongue depressors
Toothpicks
Twine
Watercolor markers
White glue
Wide-mouth straws
Wood
Yarn

Building Blocks

Elgin, Illinois  60123

# Paper, Paints Containers

## Paper

Adding machine tape
Aluminum foil
Butcher paper
Cardboard
Cardboard tubes
Coffee filters
Construction paper
Corrugated boxes
Corrugated cardboard
Crepe paper
Easel paper
Fingerpaint paper
Freezer paper
Grocery bags
Manilla paper
Newspaper
Newsprint
Paper bags
Paper plates
Pizza boards
Shelf paper
Table cloths
Wallpaper
Waxed paper
White paper
Wrapping paper

## Paints

Dry tempera
Fabric
Fingerpaint
Fluorescent tempera
Liquid tempera
Oil-based paint
Tempera cakes
Watercolor cakes
Watercolor markers
Watercolor trays

## Containers

All size meat trays
Brownie pans
Dish tubs
Ketchup/mustard squeeze bottles
Margarine tubs
Pie pans
Pitchers
Small and medium spray bottles
Soft perm bottles
Tuna cans
Unbreakable shaker bottles

Elgin, Illinois 60123

# Utensils & Textures

## Painting Utensils

Aluminum pie pans
Brayers
Casters
Coffee stir sticks
Combs
Corn cobs
Cotton swabs
Daubers
Deodorant bottles
Fly swatters
Golf balls
Hair rollers
Ice cubes
Kitchen utensils

Paint rollers
Popsicle sticks
Rolling pins
Rubber balls
Rubber fingers
Small bellows
Sponges
Spool rollers
Toothpicks
Toy vehicles
Unbreakable eyedroppers
or medicine droppers
Wallpaper seam rollers
Wide-mouth plastic
straws

## Painting Textures

Aquarium gravel
Baking powder
Cornmeal
Cornstarch
Dried coffee grounds
Kosher salt
Liquid detergent

Liquid soap
Peppercorns
Sand
Sawdust
Sugar
Whole cloves

Elgin, Illinois 60123

# Printing Props

## *Without Handles or Knobs*

Aluminum foil balls

Berry baskets

Blocks

Cardboard tubes

Cookie cutters

Corks

Corn cobs

Egg cartons

Film canisters

Funnels

Kitchen utensils

Newspaper balls

Paper cups

Spools

Styrofoam cups

Wood pieces

## *Add Handles or Knobs*

Bottle caps

Checkers

Corrugated cardboard

Dominoes

Flat keys

Jar lids

Poker chips

Pumpkin pieces

Scouring pads

Sponges

Textured fabric

Toothpicks

Twine

Elgin, Illinois 60123

# Want Ads

## Disposable Supplies

### Paper
Boxes
Cardboard
Cardboard tubes
Grocery bags
Newspaper
Wallpaper
White paper
Wrapping paper

### Containers
Margarine tubs
Meat trays
Pie pans
Pitchers
Spray bottles
Squeeze bottles
Tuna cans
Unbreakable shaker bottles

### Printing Props
Berry baskets
Bottle caps
Bottle tops
Checkers
Cookie cutters
Corks
Dominoes
Egg cartons
Film canisters
Flat keys
Jar lids
Poker chips
Spools

## Permanent Supplies
Casters
Clip-type clothespins
Cookie sheets
Film Canisters
Funnels
Gelatin molds
Gym shoes
Ice cube trays
Lazy susan plate
Packing foam
Paint rollers
Pancake turners
Plastic placemats
Plastic trays
Potato mashers
Record player
Rolling pins
Rubber balls (small)
Toaster
Toy vehicles
Warming tray
Wood

## Miscellaneous
Bedsheets
Cylinder boxes
Metal hangers
Pipe cleaners
Ribbon
Shallow boxes
Spools
Yarn

*PARENTS*
*If you have any of these items at home, please send them to school with your child. THANKS*

Elgin, Illinois 60123

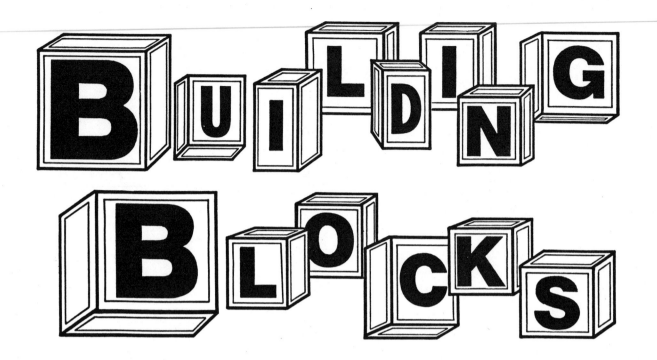

# Building Blocks Library

## The Circle Time Series

*by Liz and Dick Wilmes.* Hundreds of activities for large and small groups of children. Each book is filled with Language and Active games, Fingerplays, Songs, Stories, Snacks, and more. A great resource for every library shelf.

### Circle Time Book
Captures the spirit of 39 holidays and seasons.
**ISBN 0-943452-00-7**                **$ 9.95**

### Everyday Circle Times
Over 900 ideas. Choose from 48 topics divided into 7 sections: self-concept, basic concepts, animals, foods, science, occupations, and recreation.
**ISBN 0-943452-01-5**                **$14.95**

### More Everyday Circle Times
Divided into the same 7 sections as EVERYDAY. Features new topics such as Birds and Pizza, plus all new ideas for some familiar topics contained in EVERYDAY.
**ISBN 0-943452-14-7**                **$14.95**

### Yearful of Circle Times
52 different topics to use weekly, by seasons, or mixed throughout the year. New Friends, Signs of Fall, Snowfolk Fun, and much more.
**ISBN 0-943452-10-4**                **$14.95**

## Paint Without Brushes

*by Liz and Dick Wilmes.* Use common materials which you already have. Discover the painting possibilities in your classroom! PAINT WITHOUT BRUSHES gives your children open-ended art activities to explore paint in lots of creative ways. A valuable art resource. One you'll want to use daily.
**ISBN 0-943452-15-5**                **$12.95**

## Gifts, Cards, and Wraps

*by Wilmes and Zavodsky.* Help the children sparkle with the excitement of gift giving. Filled with thoughtful gifts, unique wraps, and special cards which the children can make and give. They're sure to bring smiles.
**ISBN 0-943452-06-6**                **$ 7.95**

## Everyday Bulletin Boards

*by Wilmes and Moehling.* Features borders, murals, backgrounds, and other open-ended art to display on your bulletin boards. Plus board ideas with patterns, which teachers can make and use to enhance their curriculum.
**ISBN 0-943452-09-0**                **$ 8.95**

## Exploring Art

*by Liz and Dick Wilmes.* EXPLORING ART is divided by months. Over 250 art ideas for paint, chalk, doughs, scissors, and more. Easy to set-up in your classroom.
**ISBN 0-943452-05-8**                **$16.95**

CIRCLE TIME

ART

## Parachute Play

*by Liz and Dick Wilmes.* A year 'round approach to one of the most versatile pieces of large muscle equipment. Starting with basic techniques, PARACHUTE PLAY provides over 100 activities to use with your parachute.
**ISBN 0-943452-03-1**                    **$ 7.95**

## Classroom Parties

*by Susan Spaete.* Each party plan suggests decorations, trimmings, and snacks which the children can easily make to set a festive mood. Choose from games, songs, art activities, stories, and related experiences which will add to the spirit and fun.
**ISBN 0-943452-07-4**                    **$ 8.95**

## Imagination Stretchers

*by Liz and Dick Wilmes.* Perfect for whole language. Over 400 conversation starters for creative discussions, simple lists, and beginning dictation and writing.
**ISBN 0-943452-04-X**                    **$ 6.95**

## Parent Programs and Open Houses

*by Susan Spaete.* Filled with a wide variety of year 'round presentations, pre-registration ideas, open houses, and end-of-the-year gatherings. All involve the children from the planning stages through the programs.
**ISBN 0-943452-08-2**                    **$ 9.95**

## Learning Centers

*by Liz and Dick Wilmes.* Hundreds of open-ended activities to quickly involve and excite your children. You'll use it every time you plan and whenever you need a quick, additional activity. A must for every teacher's bookshelf.
**ISBN 0-943452-13-9**                    **$16.95**

## Felt Board Fun

*by Liz and Dick Wilmes.* Make your felt board come alive. Discover how versatile it is as the children become involved with a wide range of activities. This unique book has over 150 ideas with accompanying patterns.
**ISBN 0-943452-02-3**                    **$14.95**

## Table & Floor Games

*by Liz and Dick Wilmes.* 32 easy-to-make, fun-to-play table/floor games with accompanying patterns ready to trace or photocopy. Teach beginning concepts such as matching, counting, colors, alphabet recognition, sorting and so on.
**ISBN 0-943452-16-3**                    **$16.95**

## Activities Unlimited

*by Adler, Caton, and Cleveland.* Create an enthusiasm for learning! Hundreds of innovative activities to help your children develop fine and gross motor skills, increase their language, become self-reliant, and play cooperatively. Whether you're a beginning teacher or a veteran, this book will quickly become one of your favorites.
**ISBN 0-943452-17-1**                    **$16.95**

# 2'S Experience Series

*by Liz and Dick Wilmes.* An exciting series developed especially for toddlers and twos!

## 2's Experience - Felt Board Fun

Make your felt board come alive. Enjoy stories, activities, and rhymes developed just for very young children. Hundreds of extra large patterns feature teddy bears, birthdays, farm animals, and much, much more.
**ISBN0-943452-19-8**                          **$12.95**

## 2's Experience - Fingerplays

A wonderful collection of easy fingerplays with accompanying games and large FINGERPLAY CARDS. Put each CARD together so that your children can look at the picture on one side, while you look at the words and actions on the other. Build a CARD file to use everyday.
**ISBN 0-943452-18-X**                          **$9.95**

## Watch for more titles in the 2's Experience series.

**A**ll books available from teacher stores, school supply catalogs or directly from:

*Thank you for your order.*

38W567 Brindlewood
Elgin, Illinois   60123
800-233-2448   708-742-1054 (FAX)